C0-ARU-580

Poems of Vision and Prophecy

Barnes & Noble Poetry Library

CHRISTMAS POEMS

LOVE POEMS

POEMS OF FUN AND FANCY

POEMS OF THE AMERICAN SPIRIT

POEMS OF VISION AND PROPHECY

Poems of Vision and Prophecy

SERIES EDITOR
David Stanford Burr

BARNES & NOBLE POETRY LIBRARY

The acknowledgments appearing on page 257 constitute an extension of this copyright page.

2002 Barnes & Noble Books

ISBN 0-7607-3314-7

Text design by Rhea Braunstein

Printed and bound in the United States of America

02 03 04 05 M 9 8 7 6 5 4 3 2

RRD-C

Contents

Foreword xi

THE BIBLE
from Ecclesiastes 1
HOMER
from Odyssey 2
RUMI
Lift Now the Lid of the Jar of Heaven 4
DANTE ALIGHIERI
Inferno, Canto III 5
SIR WALTER RALEGH
The Passionate Man's Pilgrimage 11
EDMUND SPENSER
from The Faerie Queen 14
ROBERT SOUTHWELL
The Burning Babe 18
WILLIAM SHAKESPEARE
Sonnet LV 20
"To be, or not to be, that is the question:" 21
"To-morrow, and to-morrow, and to-morrow," 23
JOHN DONNE
Holy Sonnet X 24
Song 25
The Anniversary 27
The Dreame 29
The Ecstasy 31
HENRY KING
An Exequy to His Matchless,
Never-to-Be-Forgotten Friend 34

FRANCIS QUARLES
Wherefore hidest thou thy face, and holdest me for thy enemie? 39
GEORGE HERBERT
Affliction 42
Easter Wings 45
The Pulley 46
JOHN MILTON
Il Penseroso 47
from Paradise Lost 54
RICHARD CRASHAW
An Epitaph upon Husband and Wife, which died, and were buried together 56
HENRY VAUGHAN
The Retreat 57
The World 59
They Are All Gone into the World of Light! 62
THOMAS TRAHERNE
Wonder 64
THOMAS GRAY
Elegy Written in a Country Churchyard 68
WILLIAM COLLINS
Ode on the Poetical Character 74
WILLIAM COWPER
The Castaway 78
PHILLIS WHEATLEY
An Hymn to the Morning 81
To a Lady on the Death of Her Husband 82
WILLIAM BLAKE
A Poison Tree 84
A Vision of Albion 85
A Vision of Eternity 87
Ah! Sunflower 88
Auguries of Innocence 89

London 94
The Tyger 95
ROBERT BURNS
For A' That and A' That 97
WILLIAM WORDSWORTH
Ode on Intimations of Immortality 99
The World Is Too Much with Us 108
SAMUEL TAYLOR COLERIDGE
Kubla Khan: Or a Vision in a Dream.
A Fragment 109
from The Rime of the Ancient Mariner 112
LORD BYRON
Prometheus 125
PERCY BYSSHE SHELLEY
Hymn to Intellectual Beauty 128
To a Skylark 132
JOHN KEATS
When I Have Fears 138
Ode on a Grecian Urn 139
Ode to a Nightingale 142
RALPH WALDO EMERSON
Days 146
Earth Song 147
Good-bye 149
HENRY WADSWORTH LONGFELLOW
The Day Is Done 151
The Phantom Ship 154
EDGAR ALLAN POE
Eldorado 157
The Bells 159
The Raven 164
Ulalume—A Ballad 173
ALFRED, LORD TENNYSON
The Kraken 178

from The Lady of Shalott 179
The Lotos-Eaters 182
HERMAN MELVILLE
Old Age in His Ailing 191
WALT WHITMAN
A Noiseless Patient Spider 192
As I Ebb'd with the Ocean of Life 193
Unseen Buds 198
When I Heard the Learn'd Astronomer 199
ALICE CARY
The Sea-side Cave 200
MATTHEW ARNOLD
Dover Beach 202
GEORGE MEREDITH
Lucifer in Starlight 204
EMILY DICKINSON
"Because I could not stop for Death," 205
"Departed to the judgment," 206
"I dwell in Possibility—" 207
"I felt a funeral in my brain," 208
"I never saw a moor," 209
"There's a certain slant of light," 210
CHRISTINA ROSSETTI
"Passing away, saith the World, passing away:" 211
JAMES THOMSON
from The City of Dreadful Night 213
GERARD MANLEY HOPKINS
God's Grandeur 218
WILLIAM ERNEST HENLEY
Invictus 219
EVA ROSE YORK
I Shall Not Pass This Way Again 220
LOUISE IMOGEN GUINEY
The Wild Ride 223

William Butler Yeats
The Second Coming 225
Stephen Crane
A Man Said to the Universe 226
Black Riders Came from the Sea 227
In the Desert 228
T. S. Eliot
from The Waste Land 229
Alan Seeger
I Have a Rendezvous with Death 233
Edna St. Vincent Millay
Renascence 234
Hart Crane
Proem: To Brooklyn Bridge 243
Allen Ginsberg
from Howl 246

Index of Authors 249
Index of First Lines 251
Acknowledgments 257

Foreword

Poems of Vision and Prophecy offers a broad sampling of poetic writings on the human and spiritual condition, stretching back to the Bible and Homer's mythic accounts of Odysseus's descent into the underworld nearly three thousand years ago to Allen Ginsberg's angry condemnation of late-twentieth-century American industrial capitalism, personified by Moloch.

Homer's *Odyssey,* Dante's *Divine Comedy,* Spenser's *Faerie Queen,* and Milton's *Paradise Lost*—epic invocations on the nature of man, God (or gods), departed spirits, naked maidens, and Lucifer—appear alongside the ecstasy of Rumi, the visions of Coleridge's entrancing Xanadu and haunted Ancient Mariner, and the eerie, melancholy, hallucinatory revelations in Poe's "The Raven" and "Ulalume." William Blake sees "a World in a grain of sand, / And a Heaven in a wild flower," but he also envisions a benighted nineteenth-century London. The brooding dark-night-of-the-soul ruminations in Arnold's "Dover Beach" and Eliot's *The Waste Land* are countered by the firm faith in the existence of God in Dickinson's "I never saw a moor" and in George Herbert's "Easter Wings."

Read also the uplifting and invoking words of William Ernest Henley's "Invictus"—"I am the master of my fate; / I am the captain of my soul"—and you, too, will share his vision of the "unconquerable soul," a truly visionary anthem for living our lives.

—DAVID STANFORD BURR

Poems of Vision and Prophecy

from Ecclesiastes

To every thing there is a season, and a time to
every purpose under the heaven:
A time to be born, and a time to die; a time to
plant, and a time to pluck up that which is
planted;
A time to kill, and a time to heal; a time to break
down, and a time to build up;
A time to weep, and a time to laugh; a time to
mourn, and a time to dance;
A time to cast away stones, and a time to gather
stones together; a time to embrace, and a time to
refrain from embracing;
A time to get, and a time to lose; a time to keep,
and a time to cast away;
A time to rend, and a time to sew; a time to keep
silence, and a time to speak;
A time to love, and a time to hate; a time of war,
and a time of peace.

KING JAMES VERSION

from Odyssey

from **Book XI**

"Thus in a tide of tears our sorrows flow,
And add new horror to the realms of woe;
Till side by side along the dreary coast
Advanced Achilles' and Patroclus' ghost,
A friendly pair! near these the Pylian stray'd,
And towering Ajax, an illustrious shade!
War was his joy, and pleased with loud alarms,
None but Pelides brighter shone in arms.
"Through the thick gloom his friend Achilles knew,
And as he speaks the tears descend in dew.
"'Comest thou alive to view the Stygian bounds,
Where the wan spectres walk eternal rounds;
Nor fear'st the dark and dismal waste to tread,
Throng'd with pale ghosts, familiar with the dead?'
"To whom with sighs: 'I pass these dreadful gates
To seek the Theban, and consult the Fates:
For still, distress'd, I rove from coast to coast,
Lost to my friends, and to my country lost.
But sure the eye of Time beholds no name
So bless'd as thine in all the rolls of fame;
Alive we hail'd thee with our guardian gods,
And dead thou rulest a king in these abodes.'

"'Talk not of ruling in this dolorous gloom,
Nor think vain words (he cried) can ease my doom.
Rather I'd choose laboriously to bear
A weight of woes, and breathe the vital air,
A slave to some poor hind that toils for bread,
Than reign the sceptred monarch of the dead. . . .'"

Translated from the Greek by
Alexander Pope (1688–1744)

Lift Now the Lid of the Jar of Heaven

Pour, cupbearer, the wine of the invisible,
The name and sign of what has no sign!
Pour it abundantly, it is you who enrich the soul;
Make the soul drunk, and give it wings!
Come again, always-fresh one, and teach
All our cupbearers their sacred art!
Be a spring jetting from a heart of stone!
Break the pitcher of soul and body!
Make joyful all lovers of wine!
Foment a restlessness in the heart
Of the one who thinks only of bread!
Bread's a mason of the body's prison,
Wine a rain for the garden of the soul.
I've tied the ends of the earth together,
Lift now the lid of the jar of heaven.
Close those eyes that see only faults,
Open those that contemplate the invisible
So no mosques or temples or idols remain,
So "this" or "that" is drowned in His fire.

Translated from the Persian by
Andrew Harvey (b. 1952)

Inferno, Canto III

from *THE DIVINE COMEDY*

"Through me the way is to the city dolent;
  Through me the way is to eternal dole;
  Through me the way among the people lost.
Justice incited my sublime Creator;
  Created me divine Omnipotence,
  The highest Wisdom and the primal Love.
Before me there were no created things,
  Only eterne, and I eternal last,
  All hope abandon, ye who enter in!"
These words in sombre color I beheld
  Written upon the summit of a gate;
  Whence I: "Their sense is, Master, hard to me!"
And he to me, as one experienced:
  "Here all suspicion needs must be abandoned,
  All cowardice must needs be here extinct.
We to the place have come, where I have told thee
  Thou shalt behold the people dolorous
  Who have foregone the good of intellect."
And after he had laid his hand on mine
  With joyful mien, whence I was comforted,
  He led me in among the secret things.

continues

There sighs, complaints, and ululations loud
Resounded through the air without a star,
Whence I, at the beginning, wept thereat.
Languages diverse, horrible dialects,
Accents of anger, words of agony,
And voices high and hoarse, with sound of hands,
Made up a tumult that goes whirling on
Forever in that air forever black,
Even as the sand doth, when the whirlwind
breathes.
And I, who had my head with horror bound,
Said: "Master, what is this which now I hear?
What folk is this, which seems by pain so
vanquished?"
And he to me: "This miserable mode
Maintain the melancholy souls of those
Who lived withouten infamy or praise.
Commingled are they with that caitiff choir
Of Angels, who have not rebellious been,
Nor faithful were to God, but were for self.
The heavens expelled them, not to be less fair;
Nor them the nethermore abyss receives,
For glory none the damned would have
from them."
And I: "O Master, what so grievous is
To these, that maketh them lament so sore?"
He answered: "I will tell thee very briefly.
These have no longer any hope of death;

And this blind life of theirs is so debased,
They envious are of every other fate.
No fame of them the world permits to be;
Misericord and Justice both disdain them.
Let us not speak of them, but look, and pass."
And I, who looked again, beheld a banner,
Which, whirling round, ran on so rapidly,
That of all pause it seemed to me indignant;
And after it there came so long a train
Of people, that I ne'er would have believed
That ever Death so many had undone.
When some among them I had recognized,
I looked, and I beheld the shade of him
Who made through cowardice the great refusal.
Forthwith I comprehended, and was certain,
That this the sect was of the caitiff wretches
Hateful to God and to his enemies.
These miscreants, who never were alive,
Were naked, and were stung exceedingly
By gadflies and by hornets that were there.
These did their faces irrigate with blood,
Which, with their tears commingled, at their feet
By the disgusting worms was gathered up.
And when to gazing farther I betook me,
People I saw on a great river's bank;
Whence said I: "Master, now vouchsafe to me,

continues

That I may know who these are, and what law
  Makes them appear so ready to pass over,
  As I discern athwart the dusky light."
And he to me: "These things shall all be known
  To thee, as soon as we our footsteps stay
  Upon the dismal shore of Acheron."
Then with mine eyes ashamed and downward cast,
  Fearing my words might irksome be to him,
  From speech refrained I till we reached the river.
And lo! towards us coming in a boat
  An old man, hoary with the hair of eld,
  Crying: "Woe unto you, ye souls depraved!
Hope nevermore to look upon the heavens;
  I come to lead you to the other shore,
  To the eternal shades in heat and frost.
And thou, that yonder standest, living soul,
  Withdraw thee from these people, who are dead!"
  But when he saw that I did not withdraw,
He said: "By other ways, by other ports
  Thou to the shore shalt come, not here,
    for passage;
  A lighter vessel needs must carry thee."
And unto him the Guide: "Vex thee not, Charon;
  It is so willed there where is power to do
  That which is willed; and farther question not."
Thereat were quieted the fleecy cheeks
  Of him the ferryman of the livid fen,
  Who round about his eyes had wheels of flame.

But all those souls who weary were and naked
  Their color changed and gnashed their teeth
    together,
  As soon as they had heard those cruel words.
God they blasphemed and their progenitors,
  The human race, the place, the time, the seed
  Of their engendering and of their birth!
Thereafter all together they drew back,
  Bitterly weeping, to the accursed shore,
  Which waiteth every man who fears not God.
Charon the demon, with the eyes of glede,
  Beckoning to them, collects them all together,
  Beats with his oar whoever lags behind.
As in the autumn-time the leaves fall off,
  First one and then another, till the branch
  Unto the earth surrenders all its spoils;
In similar wise the evil seed of Adam
  Throw themselves from that margin one by one,
  At signals, as a bird unto its lure.
So they depart across the dusky wave,
  And ere upon the other side they land,
  Again on this side a new troop assembles.
"My son," the courteous Master said to me,
  "All those who perish in the wrath of God
  Here meet together out of every land;

continues

And ready are they to pass o'er the river,
  Because celestial Justice spurs them on,
  So that their fear is turned into desire.
This way there never passes a good soul;
  And hence if Charon doth complain of thee,
  Well mayst thou know now what his speech
    imports."
This being finished, all the dusk champaign
  Trembled so violently, that of that terror
  The recollection bathes me still with sweat.
The land of tears gave forth a blast of wind,
  And fulminated a vermilion light,
  Which overmastered in me every sense,
And as a man whom sleep hath seized I fell.

Translated from the Italian by
Henry Wadsworth Longfellow (1807–1882)

The Passionate Man's Pilgrimage

Give me my scallop-shell of quiet,
My staff of faith to walk upon,
My scrip of joy, immortal diet,
My bottle of salvation,
My gown of glory, hope's true gage,
And thus I'll take my pilgrimage.

Blood must be my body's balmer,
No other balm will there be given,
Whilst my soul like a white palmer
Travels to the land of heaven,
Over the silver mountains,
Where spring the nectar fountains;
And there I'll kiss
The bowl of bliss,
And drink my eternal fill
On every milken hill.
My soul will be a-dry before,
But after it will ne'er thirst more;
And by the happy blissful way
More peaceful pilgrims I shall see
That have shook off their gowns of clay
And go appareled fresh like me.

stanza continues

I'll bring them first
To slake their thirst,
And then to taste those nectar suckets,
At the clear wells
Where sweetness dwells,
Drawn up by saints in crystal buckets.

And when our bottles and all we
Are filled with immortality,
Then the holy paths we'll travel,
Strewed with rubies thick as gravel,
Ceilings of diamonds, sapphire floors,
High walls of coral, and pearl bowers,
From thence to heaven's bribeless hall
Where no corrupted voices brawl,
No conscience molten into gold,
Nor forged accusers bought and sold,
No cause deferred, nor vain-spent journey,
For there Christ is the king's attorney,
Who pleads for all, without degrees,
And he hath angels, but no fees.
When the grand twelve million jury
Of our sins and sinful fury,
'Gainst our souls black verdicts give,
Christ pleads his death, and then we live.
Be thou my speaker, taintless pleader,
Unblotted lawyer, true proceeder;

stanza continues

Thou movest salvation even for alms,
Not with a bribed lawyer's palms.
And this is my eternal plea
To him that made heaven, earth, and sea,
Seeing my flesh must die so soon,
And want a head to dine next noon,
Just at the stroke when my veins start and spread,
Set on my soul an everlasting head.
Then am I ready, like a palmer fit,
To tread those blest paths which before I writ.

from The Faerie Queen

from ***Book VI, Canto X***

Vnto this place when as the Elfin Knight
  Approcht, him seemed that the merry sound
  Of a shrill pipe he playing heard on hight,
  And many feete fast thumping th'hollow ground,
  That through the woods their Eccho did rebound.
  He nigher drew, to weete what mote it be;
  There he a troupe of Ladies dauncing found
  Full merrily, and making gladfull glee,
And in the midst a Shepheard piping he did see.

He durst not enter into th'open greene,
  For dread of them vnwares to be descryde,
  For breaking of their daunce, if he were seene;
  But in the couert of the wood did byde,
  Beholding all, yet of them vnespyde.
  There he did see, that pleased much his sight,
  That euen he him selfe his eyes enuyde,
  An hundred naked maidens lilly white,
All raunged in a ring, and dauncing in delight.

All they without were raunged in a ring,
  And daunced round; but in the midst of them
  Three other Ladies did both daunce and sing,
  The whilest the rest them round about did hemme,
  And like a girlond did in compasse stemme:
  And in the middest of those same three, was placed
  Another Damzell, as a precious gemme,
  Amidst a ring most richly well enchaced,
That with her goodly presence all the rest
    much graced.

Looke how the Crowne, which *Ariadne* wore
  Vpon her yuory forehead that same day,
  That *Theseus* her vnto his bridale bore,
  When the bold *Centaures* made that bloudy fray,
  With the fierce *Lapithes*, which did them dismay;
  Being now placed in the firmament,
  Through the bright heauen doth her beams display,
  And is vnto the starres an ornament,
Which round about her moue in order excellent.

Such was the beauty of this goodly band,
  Whose sundry parts were here too long to tell:
  But she that in the midst of them did stand,
  Seem'd all the rest in beauty to excell,
  Crownd with a rosie girlond, that right well

stanza continues

Did her beseeme. And euer, as the crew
About her daunst, sweet flowres, that far did smell,
And fragrant odours they vppon her threw;
But most of all, those three did her with gifts endew.

Those were the Graces, daughters of delight,
Handmaides of *Venus*, which are wont to haunt
Vppon this hill, and daunce there day and night:
Those three to men all gifts of grace do graunt,
And all, that *Venus* in her selfe doth vaunt,
Is borrowed of them. But that faire one,
That in the midst was placed parauaunt,
Was she to whom that shepheard pypt alone,
That made him pipe so merrily, as neuer none.

She was to weete that iolly Shepheards lasse,
Which piped there vnto that merry rout,
That iolly shepheard, which there piped, was
Poore *Colin Clout* (who knowes not *Colin Clout?*)
He pypt apace, whilest they him daunst about.
Pype iolly shepheard, pype thou now apace
Vnto thy loue, that made thee low to lout:
Thy loue is present there with thee in place,
Thy loue is there aduaunst to be another Grace.

Much wondred *Calidore* at this straunge sight,
Whose like before his eye had neuer seene,
And standing long astonished in spright,
And rapt with pleasaunce, wist not what to weene;
Whether it were the traine of beauties Queene,
Or Nymphes, or Faeries, or enchaunted show,
With which his eyes mote haue deluded beene.
Therefore resoluing, what it was, to know,
Out of the wood he rose, and toward them did go.

But soone as he appeared to their vew,
They vanisht all away out of his sight,
And cleane were gone, which way he neuer knew;
All saue the shepheard, who for fell despight
Of that displeasure, broke his bag-pipe quight,
And made great mone for that vnhappy turne.
But *Calidore,* though no lesse sory wight,
For that mishap, yet seeing him to mourne,
Drew neare, that he the truth of all by him
mote learne.

The Burning Babe

As I in hoary winter's night stood shivering in the snow,
Surprised I was with sudden heat which made my heart to glow;
And lifting up a fearful eye to view what fire was near,
A pretty Babe all burning bright did in the air appear;
Who, scorched with excessive heat, such floods of tears did shed,
As though his floods should quench his flames which with his tears were fed.
"Alas!" quoth he, "but newly born in fiery heats I fry,
Yet none approach to warm their hearts or feel my fire but I.
My faultless breast the furnace is, the fuel wounding thorns;
Love is the fire, and sighs the smoke, the ashes shame and scorns;
The fuel justice layeth on, and mercy blows the coals;
The metal in this furnace wrought are men's defiled souls;

For which, as now on fire I am to work them to
their good,
So will I melt into a bath to wash them in my blood."
With this he vanished out of sight and swiftly
shrunk away,
And straight I called unto mind that it was
Christmas Day.

Sonnet LV

Not marble, nor the gilded monuments
Of princes, shall outlive this powerful rhyme;
But you shall shine more bright in these contènts
Than unswept stone, besmeared with sluttish time.
When wasteful war shall statues overturn,
And broils root out the work of masonry,
Nor Mars his sword nor war's quick fire shall burn
The living record of your memory.
'Gainst death and all-oblivious enmity
Shall you pace forth; your praise shall still find room
Even in the eyes of all posterity
That wear this world out to the ending doom.
  So, till the judgment that yourself arise,
  You live in this, and dwell in lovers' eyes.

"To be, or not to be, that is the question:"

from *HAMLET*

To be, or not to be, that is the question:
Whether 'tis nobler in the mind to suffer
The slings and arrows of outrageous fortune,
Or to take arms against a sea of troubles,
And by opposing, end them. To die, to sleep—
No more, and by a sleep to say we end
The heart-ache and the thousand natural shocks
That flesh is heir to; 'tis a consummation
Devoutly to be wish'd. To die, to sleep—
To sleep, perchance to dream—ay, there's the rub,
For in that sleep of death what dreams may come,
When we have shuffled off this mortal coil,
Must give us pause; there's the respect
That makes calamity of so long life:
For who would bear the whips and scorns of time,
Th' oppressor's wrong, the proud man's contumely,
The pangs of despis'd love, the law's delay,
The insolence of office, and the spurns
That patient merit of th' unworthy takes,
When he himself might his quietus make
With a bare bodkin; who would fardels bear,
To grunt and sweat under a weary life,

continues

But that the dread of something after death,
The undiscover'd country, from whose bourn
No traveller returns, puzzles the will,
And makes us rather bear those ills we have,
Than fly to others that we know not of?
Thus conscience does make cowards [of us all].
And thus the native hue of resolution
Is sicklied o'er with the pale cast of thought,
And enterprises of great pitch and moment
With this regard their currents turn awry,
And lose the name of action.

"To-morrow, and to-morrow, and to-morrow,"

from *MACBETH*

To-morrow, and to-morrow, and to-morrow,
Creeps in this petty pace from day to day,
To the last syllable of recorded time;
And all our yesterdays have lighted fools
The way to dusty death. Out, out, brief candle!
Life's but a walking shadow; a poor player,
That struts and frets his hour upon the stage,
And then is heard no more: it is a tale
Told by an idiot, full of sound and fury,
Signifying nothing.

WILLIAM SHAKESPEARE (1564–1616)

Holy Sonnet X

Death, be not proud, though some have called thee
Mighty and dreadful, for thou are not so;
For those whom thou think'st thou dost overthrow
Die not, poor Death, nor yet canst thou kill me.
From rest and sleep, which but thy pictures be,
Much pleasure; then from thee much more
  must flow,
And soonest our best men with thee do go,
Rest of their bones, and soul's delivery.
Thou'art slave to fate, chance, kings, and
  desperate men,
And dost with poison, war, and sickness dwell,
And poppy'or charms can make us sleep as well
And better than thy stroke; why swell'st thou then?
One short sleep past, we wake eternally,
And death shall be no more; Death, thou shalt die.

Song

Go and catch a falling star,
  Get with child a mandrake root,
Tell me where all past years are,
  Or who cleft the Devil's foot,
Teach me to hear mermaids singing,
Or to keep off envy's stinging,
    And find
    What wind
Serves to advance an honest mind.

If thou beest born to strange sights,
  Things invisible to see,
Ride ten thousand days and nights,
  Till age snow white hairs on thee,
Thou, when thou return'st, wilt tell me
All strange wonders that befell thee,
    And swear
    Nowhere
Lives a woman true, and fair.

If thou find'st one, let me know,
  Such a pilgrimage were sweet;
Yet do not, I would not go,
  Though at next door we might meet;

stanza continues

Though she were true when you met her,
And last till you write your letter,
        Yet she
        Will be
False, ere I come, to two, or three.

The Anniversary

All kings, and all their favorites,
All glory of honors, beauties, wits,
The sun itself, which makes times, as they pass,
Is elder by a year, now, than it was
When thou and I first one another saw:
All other things to their destruction draw,
Only our love hath no decay;
This, no tomorrow hath, nor yesterday;
Running it never runs from us away,
But truly keeps his first, last, everlasting day.

Two graves must hide thine and my corse;
If one might, death were no divorce.
Alas, as well as other princes, we
(Who prince enough in one another be)
Must leave at last in death, these eyes, and ears,
Oft fed with true oaths, and with sweet salt tears;
But souls where nothing dwells but love
(All other thoughts being inmates) then shall prove
This, or a love increasèd there above,
When bodies to their graves, souls from their
graves remove.

continues

And then we shall be throughly blest,
But we no more than all the rest;
Here upon earth, we're kings, and none but we
Can be such kings, nor of such subjects be;
Who is so safe as we, where none can do
Treason to us, except one of us two?
True and false fears let us refrain,
Let us love nobly, and live, and add again
Years and years unto years, till we attain
To write threescore, this is the second of our reign.

JOHN DONNE (1572–1631)

The Dreame

Deare love, for nothing lesse then thee
Would I have broke this happy dreame,
It was a theame
For reason, much too strong for phantasie,
Therefore thou wakd'st me wisely; yet
My Dreame thou brok'st not, but continued'st it,
Thou art so truth, that thoughts of thee suffice,
To make dreames truths; and fables histories;
Enter these armes, for since thou thoughtst it best,
Not to dreame all my dreame, let's act the rest.

As lightning, or a Tapers light,
Thine eyes, and not thy noise wak'd mee;
Yet I thought thee
(For thou lovest truth) an Angell, at first sight,
But when I saw thou sawest my heart,
And knew'st my thoughts, beyond an Angels art,
When thou knew'st what I dreamt, when thou knew'st when
Excesse of joy would wake me, and cam'st then,
I doe confesse, it could not chuse but bee
Prophane, to thinke thee any thing but thee.

continues

Comming and staying show'd thee, thee,
But rising makes me doubt, that now,
    Thou art not thou.
That love is weake, where feare's as strong as hee;
'Tis not all spirit, pure, and brave,
If mixture it of *Feare, Shame, Honor,* have;
Perchance as torches which must ready bee,
Men light and put out, so thou deal'st with mee,
Thou cam'st to kindle, goest to come; Then I
Will dreame that hope againe, but else would die.

The Ecstasy

Where, like a pillow on a bed,
  A pregnant bank swelled up to rest
The violet's reclining head,
  Sat we two, one another's best.
Our hands were firmly cèmented
  With a fast balm, which thence did spring.
Our eye-beams twisted, and did thread
  Our eyes upon one double string;
So to'intergraft our hands, as yet
  Was all the means to make us one,
And pictures in our eyes to get
  Was all our propagation.
As 'twixt two equal armies, Fate
  Suspends uncertain victory,
Our souls (which to advance their state,
  Were gone out) hung 'twixt her and me.
And whilst our souls negotiate there,
  We like sepulchral statues lay;
All day the same our postures were,
  And we said nothing all the day.
If any, so by love refined
  That he soul's language understood,
And by good love were grown all mind,
  Within convenient distance stood,

continues

He (though he knew not which soul spake,
  Because both meant, both spake the same)
Might thence a new concoction take,
  And part far purer than he came.
This ecstasy doth unperplex,
  We said, and tell us what we love;
We see by this it was not sex;
  We see we saw not what did move;
But as all several souls contain
  Mixture of things, they know not what,
Love these mixed souls doth mix again,
  And makes both one, each this and that.
A single violet transplant,
  The strength, the color, and the size
(All which before was poor, and scant)
  Redoubles still, and multiplies.
When love, with one another so
  Interinanimates two souls,
That abler soul, which thence doth flow,
  Defects of loneliness controls.
We then, who are this new soul, know,
  Of what we are composed, and made,
For, th' atomies of which we grow,
  Are souls, whom no change can invade.
But O alas, so long, so far
  Our bodies why do we forbear?
They're ours, though they're not we; we are
  Th' intelligences, they the spheres.

We owe them thanks because they thus
  Did us to us at first convey,
Yielded their forces, sense, to us,
  Nor are dross to us, but allay.
On man heaven's influence works not so,
  But that it first imprints the air,
So soul into the soul may flow,
  Though it to body first repair.
As our blood labors to beget
  Spirits like souls as it can,
Because such fingers need to knit
  That subtle knot which makes us man:
So must pure lovers' souls descend
  To'affections, and to faculties,
Which sense may reach and apprehend;
  Else a great Prince in prison lies.
To'our bodies turn we then, that so
  Weak men on love revealed may look;
Love's mysteries in souls do grow,
  But yet the body is his book.
And if some lover, such as we,
  Have heard this dialogue of one,
Let him still mark us; he shall see
  Small change when we're to bodies gone.

An Exequy to His Matchless, Never-to-Be-Forgotten Friend

Accept, thou shrine of my dead saint,
Instead of dirges, this complaint;
And for sweet flowers to crown thy hearse,
Receive a strew of weeping verse
From thy grieved friend, whom thou might'st see
Quite melted into tears for thee,

Dear loss! since thy untimely fate
My task hath been to meditate
On thee, on thee; thou art the book,
The library whereon I look,
Though almost blind. For thee, loved clay,
I languish out, not live, the day,
Using no other exercise
But what I practice with mine eyes;
By which wet glasses I find out
How lazily time creeps about
To one that mourns: this, only this,
My exercise and business is.
So I compute the weary hours
With sighs dissolvèd into showers.

Nor wonder if my time go thus
Backward and most preposterous;

stanza continues

Thou hast benighted me, thy set
This eve of blackness did beget,
Who wast my day, though overcast
Before thou hadst thy noontide passed;
And I remember must in tears,
Thou scarce hadst seen so many years
As day tells hours. By thy clear sun
My love and fortune first did run;
But thou wilt never more appear
Folded within my hemisphere,
Since both thy light and motiòn
Like a fled star is fallen and gone;
And 'twixt me and my soul's dear wish
An earth now interposèd is,
Which such a strange eclipse doth make
As ne'er was read in almanac.

I could allow thee for a time
To darken me and my sad clime;
Were it a month, a year, or ten,
I would thy exile live till then,
And all that space my mirth adjourn,
So thou wouldst promise to return;
And putting off thy ashy shroud,
At length disperse this sorrow's cloud.

continues

But woe is me! the longest date
Too narrow is to calculate
These empty hopes; never shall I
Be so much blest as to descry
A glimpse of thee, till that day come
Which shall the earth to cinders doom,
And a fierce fever must calcine
The body of this world—like thine,
My little world! That fit of fire
Once off, our bodies shall aspire
To our souls' bliss; then we shall rise
And view ourselves with clearer eyes
In that calm region where no night
Can hide us from each other's sight.

Meantime, thou hast her, earth: much good
May my harm do thee. Since it stood
With heaven's will I might not call
Her longer mine, I give thee all
My short-lived right and interest
In her whom living I loved best;
With a most free and bounteous grief
I give thee what I could not keep.
Be kind to her, and prithee look
Thou write into thy doomsday book
Each parcel of this rarity
Which in thy casket shrined doth lie.

stanza continues

See that thou make thy reckoning straight,
And yield her back again by weight;
For thou must audit on thy trust
Each grain and atom of this dust,
As thou wilt answer him that lent,
Not gave thee, my dear monument.

So close the ground, and 'bout her shade
Black curtains draw; my bride is laid.

Sleep on, my love, in thy cold bed,
Never to be disquieted!
My last good-night! Thou wilt not wake
Till I thy fate shall overtake;
Till age, or grief, or sickness must
Marry my body to that dust
It so much loves; and fill the room
My heart keeps empty in thy tomb.
Stay for me there; I will not fail
To meet thee in that hollow vale.
And think not much of my delay;
I am already on the way,
And follow thee with all the speed
Desire can make, or sorrows breed.
Each minute is a short degree,
And every hour a step towards thee.

stanza continues

At night when I betake to rest,
Next morn I rise nearer my west
Of life, almost by eight hours' sail,
Than when sleep breathed his drowsy gale.

Thus from the sun my bottom steers,
And my day's compass downward bears;
Nor labor I to stem the tide
Through which to thee I swiftly glide.

'Tis true, with shame and grief I yield,
Thou like the van first took'st the field,
And gotten hast the victory
In thus adventuring to die
Before me, whose more years might crave
A just precèdence in the grave.
But hark! my pulse like a soft drum
Beats my approach, tells thee I come;
And slow howe'er my marches be,
I shall at last sit down by thee.

The thought of this bids me go on,
And wait my dissolutiòn.
With hope and comfort. Dear (forgive
The crime), I am content to live
Divided, with but half a heart,
Till we shall meet, and never part.

Wherefore hidest thou thy face, and holdest me for thy enemie?

Why dost thou shade thy lovely face? O why
Does that ecclipsing hand, so long, deny
The Sun-shine of thy soule-enliv'ning eye?

Without that Light, what light remaines in me?
Thou art my Life, my Way, my Light; in Thee
I live, I move, and by thy beames I see.

Thou art my Life; If thou but turne away,
My life's a thousand deaths: thou art my Way;
Without thee, Lord, I travell not, but stray.

My Light thou art; without thy glorious sight,
Mine eyes are darkned with perpetuall night.
My God, thou art my Way, my Life, my Light.

Thou art my Way; I wander, if thou flie:
Thou art my Light; if hid, how blind am I!
Thou art my Life; if thou withdraw, I die.

Mine eyes are blind and darke; I cannot see;
To whom, or whither should my darknesse flee,
But to the Light? And who's that Light but Thee?

continues

My path is lost; my wandring steps do stray;
I cannot safely go, nor safely stay;
Whom should I see but Thee, my Path my Way?

O, I am dead: to whom shall I, poore I,
Repaire? to whom shall my sad Ashes fly
But Life? And where is Life but in thine eye?

And yet thou turn'st away thy face, and fly'st me;
And yet I sue for Grace and thou deny'st me;
Speake, art thou angry, Lord, or onely try'st me?

Unskreene those heav'nly lamps, or tell me why
Thou shad'st thy face. Perhaps, thou thinkst, no eye
Can view those flames, and not drop downe and die.

If that be all, shine forth, and draw thee nigher;
Let me behold and die; for my desire
Is Phoenix-like to perish in that Fire.

Death-conquer'd Laz'rus was redeem'd by Thee;
If I am dead, Lord, set death's pris'ner free;
Am I more spent, or stink I worse than he?

If my pufft light be out, give leave to tine
My flameless snuffle at that bright Lamp of thine;
O what's thy Light the lesse for lighting mine?

If I have lost my Path, great Shepheard, say,
Shall I still wander in a doubtfull way?
Lord, shall a Lamb of Isr'el's sheepfold stray?

Thou art the Pilgrim's Path: the blind man's Eye;
The dead man's Life; on thee my hopes rely;
If thou remove, I erre; I grope; I die.

Disclose thy Sun beames; close thy wings, and stay;
See, see, how I am blind, and dead, and stray,
O thou, that art my Light, my Life, my Way.

Affliction

When first thou didst entice to thee my heart,
    I thought the service brave:
So many joys I writ down for my part,
    Besides what I might have
Out of my stock of natural delights,
Augmented with thy gracious benefits.

I lookèd on thy furniture so fine,
    And made it fine to me;
Thy glorious household stuff did me entwine,
    And 'tice me unto thee.
Such stars I counted mine: both heaven and earth
Paid me my wages in a world of mirth.

What pleasures could I want, whose king I served,
    Where joys my fellows were?
Thus argued into hopes, my thoughts reserved
    No place for grief or fear;
Therefore my sudden soul caught at the place,
And made her youth and fierceness seek thy face:

At first thou gav'st me milk and sweetnesses;
    I had my wish and way:
My days were strawed with flowers and happiness;
    There was no month but May.
But with my years sorrow did twist and grow.
And made a party unawares for woe.

My flesh began unto my soul in pain,
        "Sicknesses cleave my bones;
Consuming agues dwell in every vein,
        And tune my breath to groans."
Sorrow was all my soul; I scarce believed,
Till grief did tell me roundly, that I lived.

When I got health, thou took'st away my life,
        And more; for my friends die:
My mirth and edge was lost: a blunted knife
        Was of more use than I.
Thus thin and lean without a fence or friend,
I was blown through with ev'ry storm and wind.

Whereas my birth and spirit rather took
        The way that takes the town,
Thou didst betray me to a lingering book,
        And wrap me in a gown.
I was entangled in the world of strife,
Before I had the power to change my life.

Yet, for I threatened oft the siege to raise,
        Not simpering all mine age,
Thou often didst with academic praise
        Melt and dissolve my rage.
I took thy sweetened pill, till I came where
I could not go away, nor persevere.

continues

Yet lest perchance I should too happy be
    In my unhappiness,
Turning my purge to food, thou throwest me
    Into more sicknesses.
Thus doth thy power cross-bias me, not making
Thine own gift good, yet me from my ways taking.

Now I am here, what thou wilt do with me
    None of my books will show:
I read, and sigh, and wish I were a tree,
    For sure then I should grow
To fruit or shade; at least, some bird would trust
Her household to me, and I should be just.

Yet, though thou troublest me, I must be meek;
    In weakness must be stout:
Well, I will change the service, and go seek
    Some other master out.
Ah, my dear God! though I am clean forgot,
Let me not love thee, if I love thee not.

Easter Wings

Lord, Who createdst man in wealth and store,
Though foolishly he lost the same,
Decaying more and more,
Till he became
Most poore:
With Thee
O let me rise,
As larks, harmoniously,
And sing this day Thy victories:
Then shall the fall further the flight in me.

My tender age in sorrow did beginne;
And still with sicknesses and shame
Thou didst so punish sinne,
That I became
Most thinne.
With Thee
Let me combine,
And feel this day Thy victorie;
For, if I imp my wing on Thine,
Affliction shall advance the flight in me.

The Pulley

When God at first made man,
Having a glass of blessings standing by,
"Let us," said he, "pour on him all we can.
Let the world's riches, which dispersèd lie,
Contract into a span."

So strength first made a way;
Then beauty flowed, then wisdom, honor, pleasure.
When almost all was out, God made a stay,
Perceiving that, alone of all his treasure,
Rest in the bottom lay.

"For if I should," said he,
"Bestow this jewel also on my creature,
He would adore my gifts instead of me,
And rest in Nature, not the God of Nature;
So both should losers be.

"Yet let him keep the rest,
But keep them with repining restlessness.
Let him be rich and weary, that at least,
If goodness lead him not, yet weariness
May toss him to my breast."

GEORGE HERBERT (1593–1633)

Il Penseroso

Hence vain deluding Joys,
  The brood of Folly without father bred.
How little you bestead,
  Or fill the fixèd mind with all your toys;
Dwell in some idle brain,
  And fancies fond with gaudy shapes possess,
As thick and numberless
  As the gay motes that people the sunbeams,
Or likest hovering dreams,
  The fickle pensioners of Morpheus' train.
But hail thou Goddess, sage and holy,
Hail, divinest Melancholy,
Whose saintly visage is too bright
To hit the sense of human sight;
And therefore to our weaker view,
O'erlaid with black, staid Wisdom's hue.
Black, but such as in esteem,
Prince Memnon's sister might beseem,
Or that starred Ethiope queen that strove
To set her beauty's praise above
The sea nymphs, and their powers offended.
Yet thou art higher far descended;
Thee bright-haired Vesta long of yore
To solitary Saturn bore;

continues

His daughter she (in Saturn's reign
Such mixture was not held a stain).
Oft in glimmering bowers and glades
He met her, and in secret shades
Of woody Ida's inmost grove,
While yet there was no fear of Jove.
Come pensive nun, devout and pure,
Sober, steadfast, and demure,
All in a robe of darkest grain,
Flowing with majestic train,
And sable stole of cypress lawn
Over thy decent shoulders drawn.
Come, but keep thy wonted state,
With even step and musing gait,
And looks commercing with the skies,
Thy rapt soul sitting in thine eyes:
There held in holy passion still,
Forget thyself to marble, till
With a sad leaden downward cast,
Thou fix them on the earth as fast.
And join with thee calm Peace and Quiet,
Spare Fast, that oft with gods doth diet,
And hears the Muses in a ring
Aye round about Jove's altar sing.
And add to these retired Leisure,
That in trim gardens takes his pleasure;
But first, and chiefest, with thee bring,
Him that yon soars on golden wing,

Guiding the fiery-wheelèd throne,
The cherub Contemplation;
And the mute Silence hist along
'Less Philomel will deign a song,
In her sweetest, saddest plight,
Smoothing the rugged brow of night,
While Cynthia checks her dragon yoke
Gently o'er th' accustomed oak;
Sweet bird that shunn'st the noise of folly,
Most musical, most melancholy!
Thee chantress oft the woods among,
I woo to hear thy evensong;
And missing thee, I walk unseen
On the dry smooth-shaven green,
To behold the wandering moon,
Riding near her highest noon,
Like one that had been led astray
Through the Heaven's wide pathless way;
And oft as if her head she bowed,
Stooping through a fleecy cloud.
Oft on a plat of rising ground,
I hear the far-off curfew sound,
Over some wide-watered shore,
Swinging slow with sullen roar;
Or if the air will not permit,
Some still removèd place will fit,

continues

Where glowing embers through the room
Teach light to counterfeit a gloom
Far from all resort of mirth,
Save the cricket on the hearth,
Or the bellman's drowsy charm,
To bless the doors from nightly harm;
Or let my lamp at midnight hour
Be seen in some high lonely tower,
Where I may oft outwatch the Bear,
With thrice great Hermes, or unsphere
The spirit of Plato to unfold
What worlds, or what vast regions hold
The immortal mind that hath forsook
Her mansion in this fleshly nook;
And of those demons that are found
In fire, air, flood, or underground,
Whose power hath a true consent
With planet, or with element.
Some time let gorgeous Tragedy
In sceptered pall come sweeping by,
Presenting Thebes, or Pelops' line,
Or the tale of Troy divine.
Or what (though rare) of later age
Ennobled hath the buskined stage.
But, O sad virgin, that thy power
Might raise Musaeus from his bower,
Or bid the soul of Orpheus sing
Such notes as, warbled to the string,

Drew iron tears down Pluto's cheek,
And made Hell grant what Love did seek.
Or call up him that left half told
The story of Cambuscan bold,
Of Camball, and of Algarsife,
And who had Canacee to wife,
That owned the virtuous ring and glass,
And of the wondrous horse of brass,
On which the Tartar king did ride;
And if aught else great bards beside
In sage and solemn tunes have sung,
Of tourneys and of trophies hung,
Of forests and enchantments drear,
Where more is meant than meets the ear.
Thus, Night, oft see me in thy pale career,
Till civil-suited morn appear,
Not tricked and frounced as she was wont,
With the Attic boy to hunt,
But kerchiefed in a comely cloud,
While rocking winds are piping loud,
Or ushered with a shower still,
When the gust hath blown his fill,
Ending on the rustling leaves,
With minute-drops from off the eaves.
And when the sun begins to fling
His flaring beams, me, Goddess, bring

continues

To archèd walks of twilight groves,
And shadows brown that Sylvan loves
Of pine or monumental oak,
Where the rude ax with heavèd stroke,
Was never heard the nymphs to daunt,
Or fright them from their hallowed haunt.
There in close covert by some brook,
Where no profaner eye may look,
Hide me from day's garish eye,
While the bee with honeyed thigh,
That at her flowery work doth sing,
And the waters murmuring
With such consort as they keep,
Entice the dewy-feathered sleep;
And let some strange mysterious dream,
Wave at his wings in airy stream,
Of lively portraiture displayed,
Softly on my eyelids laid.
And as I wake, sweet music breathe
Above, about, or underneath,
Sent by some spirit to mortals good,
Or th' unseen genius of the wood.
But let my due feet never fail
To walk the studious cloister's pale,
And love the high embowèd roof,
With antic pillars massy proof,
And storied windows richly dight,
Casting a dim religious light.

There let the pealing organ blow,
To the full-voiced choir below,
In service high, and anthems clear,
As may with sweetness, through mine ear,
Dissolve me into ecstasies,
And bring all heaven before mine eyes.
And may at last my weary age
Find out the peaceful hermitage,
The hairy gown and mossy cell,
Where I may sit and rightly spell
Of every star that Heaven doth show,
And every herb that sips the dew
Till old experience do attain
To something like prophetic strain.
These pleasures, Melancholy, give,
And I with thee will choose to live.

from Paradise Lost

from **Book I**

"Is this the Region, this the Soil, the Clime,"
Said then the lost Arch Angel, "this the seat
That we must change for Heav'n, this mournful
gloom
For that celestial light? Be it so, since hee
Who now is Sovran can dispose and bid
What shall be right: farthest from him is best
Whom reason hath equall'd, force hath made supreme
Above his equals. Farewell happy Fields
Where Joy for ever dwells: Hail horrors, hail
Infernal world, and thou profoundest Hell
Receive thy new Possessor: One who brings
A mind not to be chang'd by Place or Time.
The mind is its own place, and in itself
Can make a Heav'n of Hell, a Hell of Heav'n.
What matter where, if I be still the same,
And what I should be, all but less than hee
Whom Thunder hath made greater? Here at least
We shall be free; th'Almighty hath not built
Here for his envy, will not drive us hence:
Here we may reign secure, and in my choice
To reign is worth ambition though in Hell:
Better to reign in Hell, than serve in Heav'n.
But wherefore let we then our faithful friends,

Th'associates and co-partners of our loss
Lie thus astonisht on th'oblivious Pool,
And call them not to share with us their part
In this unhappy Mansion, or once more
With rallied Arms to try what may be yet
Regain'd in Heav'n, or what more lost in Hell?"

An Epitaph upon Husband and Wife, which died, and were buried together

To these, whom Death again did wed,
This grave 's the second Marriage-bed.
For though the hand of Fate could force
'Twixt Soul and Body a Divorce,
It could not sunder man and wife,
'Cause they both lived but one life.
Peace, good Reader. Doe not weep.
Peace, the Lovers are asleep.
They, sweet Turtles, folded lie
In the last knot Love could tie.
And though they lie as they were dead,
Their pillow stone, their sheetes of lead
(Pillow hard, and sheets not warm)
Love made the bed; they'll take no harm.
Let them sleep: let them sleep on,
Till this stormy night be gone,
Till the Æternal morrow dawn;
Then the curtaines will be drawn
And they wake into a light
Whose day shall never die in Night.

The Retreat

Happy those early days! when I
Shined in my angel infancy.
Before I understood this place
Appointed for my second race,
Or taught my soul to fancy aught
But a white, celestial thought;
When yet I had not walked above
A mile or two from my first love,
And looking back, at that short space,
Could see a glimpse of His bright face;
When on some gilded cloud or flower
My gazing soul would dwell an hour,
And in those weaker glories spy
Some shadows of eternity;
Before I taught my tongue to wound
My conscience with a sinful sound,
Or had the black art to dispense
A several sin to every sense,
But felt through all this fleshly dress
Bright shoots of everlastingness.
O, how I long to travel back,
And tread again that ancient track!
That I might once more reach that plain
Where first I left my glorious train,

continues

From whence th' enlightened spirit sees
That shady city of palm trees.
But, ah! my soul with too much stay
Is drunk, and staggers in the way.
Some men a forward motion love;
But I by backward steps would move,
And when this dust falls to the urn,
In that state I came, return.

The World

I saw Eternity the other night
Like a great Ring of pure and endless light,
All calm, as it was bright,
And round beneath it, Time in hours, days, years
Driv'n by the spheres
Like a vast shadow mov'd, In which the world
And all her train were hurl'd;
The doting Lover in his queintest strain
Did there Complain,
Neer him, his Lute, his fancy, and his flights,
Wits sour delights,
With gloves, and knots the silly snares of pleasure;
Yet his dear Treasure
All scatter'd lay, while he his eyes did pour
Upon a flowr.

The darksome States-man, hung with weights and woe,
Like a thick midnight-fog mov'd there so slow
He did nor stay, nor go;
Condemning thoughts (like sad Ecclipses) scowl
Upon his soul,
And Clouds of crying witnesses without
Pursued him with one shout.

stanza continues

Yet digg'd the Mole, and lest his ways be found
Workt under ground,
Where he did Clutch his prey, but one did see
That policie;
Churches and altars fed him, Perjuries
Were gnats and flies,
It rain'd about him blood and tears, but he
Drank them as free.

The fearfull miser on a heap of rust
Sate pining all his life there, did scarce trust
His own hands with the dust,
Yet would not place one peece above, but lives
In feare of theeves.
Thousands there were as frantick as himself
And hugg'd each one his pelf,
The down-right Epicure plac'd heav'n in sense
And scorned pretence
While others slipt into a wide Excesse
Said little lesse;
The weaker sort slight, triviall wares inslave
Who think them brave,
And poor, despised truth sate Counting by
Their victory.

Yet some, who all this while did weep and sing,
And sing, and weep, soar'd up into the Ring,
    But most would use no wing.
O fools (said I,) thus to prefer dark night
        Before true light,
To live in grots, and caves, and hate the day
    Because it shews the way,
The way which from this dead and dark abode
        Leads up to God,
A way where you might tread the Sun, and be
        More bright than he.
But as I did their madness so discusse
        One whisper'd thus,
This Ring the Bride-groome did for none provide
        But for his bride.

They Are All Gone into the World of Light!

They are all gone into the world of light!
  And I alone sit lingering here;
Their very memory is fair and bright,
  And my sad thoughts doth clear.

It glows and glitters in my cloudy breast
  Like stars upon some gloomy grove,
Or those faint beams in which this hill is dressed
  After the sun's remove.

I see them walking in an air of glory,
  Whose light doth trample on my days;
My days, which are at best but dull and hoary,
  Mere glimmering and decays.

O holy hope! and high humility,
  High as the heavens above!
These are your walks, and you have showed them me
  To kindle my cold love.

Dear, beauteous death! the jewel of the just,
  Shining nowhere but in the dark;
What mysteries do lie beyond thy dust,
  Could man outlook that mark!

HENRY VAUGHAN (1622?–1695)

He that hath found some fledged bird's nest
    may know
  At first sight if the bird be flown;
But what fair well or grove he sings in now,
  That is to him unknown.

And yet, as angels in some brighter dreams
  Call to the soul when man doth sleep,
So some strange thoughts transcend our
    wonted themes,
  And into glory peep.

If a star were confined into a tomb,
  Her captive flames must needs burn there;
But when the hand that locked her up gives room,
  She'll shine through all the sphere.

O Father of eternal life, and all
  Created glories under Thee!
Resume Thy spirit from this world of thrall
  Into true liberty!

Either disperse these mists, which blot and fill
  My perspective still as they pass;
Or else remove me hence unto that hill
  Where I shall need no glass.

Wonder

1

How like an Angel came I down!
How Bright are all Things here!
When first among his Works I did appear
O how their GLORY me did Crown?
The World resembled his *Eternitie,*
In which my Soul did Walk;
And evry Thing that I did see,
Did with me talk.

2

The Skies in their Magnificence,
The Lively, Lovely Air;
Oh how Divine, how Soft, how Sweet, how fair!
The Stars did entertain my Sence,
And all the Works of GOD so Bright and pure,
So Rich and Great did seem,
As if they ever must endure,
In my Esteem.

3

A Native Health and Innocence
Within my Bones did grow,
And while my GOD did all his Glories shew,

stanza continues

I felt a Vigour in my Sence
That was all SPIRIT. I within did flow
With Seas of Life, like Wine;
I nothing in the World did know,
But 'twas Divine.

4

Harsh ragged Objects were conceald,
Oppressions Tears and Cries,
Sins, Griefs, Complaints, Dissentions, Weeping Eys,
Were hid: and only Things reveald,
Which Heav'nly Spirits, and the Angels prize.
The State of Innocence
And Bliss, not Trades and Poverties,
Did fill my Sence.

5

The Streets were pavd with Golden Stones,
The Boys and Girles were mine,
Oh how did all their Lovly faces shine!
The Sons of Men were Holy Ones.
In Joy, and Beauty, then appear'd to me,
And evry Thing which here I found,
While like an Angel I did See,
Adornd the Ground.

continues

6

Rich Diamond and Pearl and Gold
In evry Place was seen;
Rare Splendors, Yellow, Blew, Red, White and Green,
Mine Eys did evry where behold.
Great Wonders clothd with Glory did appear,
Amazement was my Bliss.
That and my Wealth was evry where:
No Joy to this!

7

Cursd and Devisd Proprieties,
With Envy, Avarice
And Fraud, those Feinds that Spöyl even Paradice,
Fled from the Splendor of mine Eys.
And so did Hedges, Ditches, Limits, Bounds,
I dreamd not ought of those,
But wanderd over all mens Grounds,
And found Repose.

8

Proprieties themselvs were mine,
And Hedges Ornaments;
Walls, Boxes, Coffers, and their rich Contents
Did not Divide my Joys, but all combine.

stanza continues

Clothes, Ribbans, Jewels, Laces, I esteemd
My Joys by others worn;
For me they all to wear them seemd
When I was born.

Elegy Written in a Country Churchyard

The curfew tolls the knell of parting day,
The lowing herd wind slowly o'er the lea,
The plowman homeward plods his weary way,
And leaves the world to darkness and to me.

Now fades the glimmering landscape on the sight,
And all the air a solemn stillness holds,
Save where the beetle wheels his droning flight,
And drowsy tinklings lull the distant folds;

Save that from yonder ivy-mantled tower
The moping owl does to the moon complain
Of such, as wandering near her secret bower,
Molest her ancient solitary reign.

Beneath those rugged elms, that yew tree's shade,
Where heaves the turf in many a moldering heap,
Each in his narrow cell forever laid,
The rude forefathers of the hamlet sleep.

The breezy call of incense-breathing morn,
The swallow twittering from the straw-built shed,
The cock's shrill clarion, or the echoing horn,
No more shall rouse them from their lowly bed.

 THOMAS GRAY (1716–1771)

For them no more the blazing hearth shall burn,
Or busy housewife ply her evening care;
No children run to lisp their sire's return,
Or climb his knees the envied kiss to share.

Oft did the harvest to their sickle yield,
Their furrow oft the stubborn glebe has broke;
How jocund did they drive their team afield!
How bowed the woods beneath their sturdy
stroke!

Let not Ambition mock their useful toil,
Their homely joys, and destiny obscure;
Nor Grandeur hear with a disdainful smile
The short and simple annals of the poor.

The boast of heraldry, the pomp of power,
And all that beauty, all that wealth e'er gave,
Awaits alike the inevitable hour.
The paths of glory lead but to the grave.

Nor you, ye proud, impute to these the fault,
If Memory o'er their tomb no trophies raise,
Where through the long-drawn aisle and fretted
vault
The pealing anthem swells the note of praise.

continues

Can storied urn or animated bust
  Back to its mansion call the fleeting breath?
Can Honor's voice provoke the silent dust,
  Or Flattery soothe the dull cold ear of Death?

Perhaps in this neglected spot is laid
  Some heart once pregnant with celestial fire;
Hands that the rod of empire might have swayed,
  Or waked to ecstasy the living lyre.

But Knowledge to their eyes her ample page
  Rich with the spoils of time did ne'er unroll;
Chill Penury repressed their noble rage,
  And froze the genial current of the soul.

Full many a gem of purest ray serene,
  The dark unfathomed caves of ocean bear:
Full many a flower is born to blush unseen,
  And waste its sweetness on the desert air.

Some village Hampden, that with dauntless breast
  The little tyrant of his fields withstood;
Some mute inglorious Milton here may rest,
  Some Cromwell guiltless of his country's blood.

The applause of listening senates to command,
  The threats of pain and ruin to despise,
To scatter plenty o'er a smiling land,
  And read their history in a nation's eyes,

Their lot forbade: nor circumscribed alone
  Their growing virtues, but their crimes confined;
Forbade to wade through slaughter to a throne,
  And shut the gates of mercy on mankind,

The struggling pangs of conscious truth to hide,
  To quench the blushes of ingenuous shame,
Or heap the shrine of Luxury and Pride
  With incense kindled at the Muse's flame.

Far from the madding crowd's ignoble strife,
  Their sober wishes never learned to stray;
Along the cool sequestered vale of life
  They kept the noiseless tenor of their way.

Yet even these bones from insult to protect
  Some frail memorial still erected nigh,
With uncouth rhymes and shapeless sculpture
    decked,
  Implores the passing tribute of a sigh.

Their name, their years, spelt by the unlettered
    Muse,
  The place of fame and elegy supply:
And many a holy text around she strews,
  That teach the rustic moralist to die.

continues

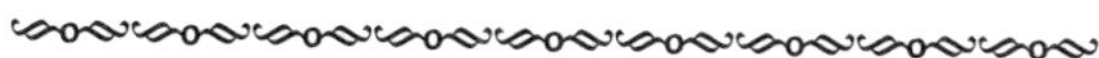

For who to dumb Forgetfulness a prey,
  This pleasing anxious being e'er resigned,
Left the warm precincts of the cheerful day,
  Nor cast one longing lingering look behind?

On some fond breast the parting soul relies,
  Some pious drops the closing eye requires;
Even from the tomb the voice of Nature cries,
  Even in our ashes live their wonted fires.

For thee, who mindful of the unhonored dead
  Dost in these lines their artless tale relate;
If chance, by lonely contemplation led,
  Some kindred spirit shall inquire thy fate,

Haply some hoary-headed swain may say,
  "Oft have we seen him at the peep of dawn
Brushing with hasty steps the dews away
  To meet the sun upon the upland lawn.

"There at the foot of yonder nodding beech
  That wreathes its old fantastic roots so high,
His listless length at noontide would he stretch,
  And pore upon the brook that babbles by.

"Hard by yon wood, now smiling as in scorn,
  Muttering his wayward fancies he would rove,
Now drooping, woeful wan, like one forlorn,
  Or crazed with care, or crossed in hopeless love.

"One morn I missed him on the customed hill,
Along the heath and near his favorite tree;
Another came; nor yet beside the rill,
Nor up the lawn, nor at the wood was he;

"The next with dirges due in sad array
Slow through the churchway path we saw
him borne.
Approach and read (for thou canst read) the lay,
Graved on the stone beneath yon aged thorn."

The Epitaph

Here rests his head upon the lap of Earth
A youth to Fortune and to Fame unknown.
Fair Science frowned not on his humble birth,
And Melancholy marked him for her own.

Large was his bounty, and his soul sincere,
Heaven did a recompense as largely send:
He gave to Misery all he had, a tear,
He gained from Heaven ('twas all he wished) a friend.

No farther seek his merits to disclose,
Or draw his frailties from their dread abode
(There they alike in trembling hope repose),
The bosom of his Father and his God.

Ode on the Poetical Character

Strophe

As once, if not with light regard,
I read aright that gifted bard
(Him whose school above the rest
His loveliest Elfin Queen has blest).
One, only one, unrivaled fair,
Might hope the magic girdle wear,
At solemn tourney hung on high,
The wish of each love-darting eye;
Lo! to each other nymph in turn applied,
  As if, in air unseen, some hovering hand,
Some chaste and angel-friend to virgin-fame,
  With whispered spell had burst the starting band,
It left unblest her loathed dishonored side;
  Happier, hopeless fair, if never
  Her baffled hand with vain endeavor
Had touched that fatal zone to her denied!
Young Fancy thus, to me divinest name,
  To whom, prepared and bathed in Heaven
  The cest of amplest power is given;
  To few the godlike gift assigns,
  To gird their blest, prophetic loins,
And gaze her visions wild, and feel unmixed
    her flame!

Epode

The band, as fairy legends say,
Was wove on that creating day,
When He, who called with thought to birth
Yon tented sky, this laughing earth,
And dressed with springs, and forests tall,
And poured the main engirting all,
Long by the loved Enthusiast wooed,
Himself in some diviner mood,
Retiring, sate with her alone,
And placed her on his sapphire throne;
The whiles, the vaulted shrine around,
Seraphic wires were heard to sound,
Now sublimest triumph swelling,
Now on love and mercy dwelling;
And she, from out the veiling cloud,
Breathed her magic notes aloud:
And thou, thou rich-haired Youth of Morn,
And all thy subject life was born!
The dangerous Passions kept aloof,
Far from the sainted growing woof;
But near it sate ecstatic Wonder,
Listening the deep applauding thunder;
And Truth, in sunny vest arrayed,
By whose the tarsel's eyes were made;

stanza continues

All the shadowy tribes of Mind,
In braided dance their murmurs joined,
And all the bright uncounted Powers
Who feed on Heaven's ambrosial flowers.
Where is the bard, whose soul can now
Its high presuming hopes avow?
Where he who thinks, with rapture blind,
This hallow'd work for him designed?

Antistrophe

High on some cliff, to Heaven up-piled,
Of rude access, of prospect wild,
Where, tangled round the jealous steep,
Strange shades o'erbrow the valleys deep,
And holy Genii guard the rock,
Its glooms embrown, its springs unlock,
While on its rich ambitious head,
An Eden, like his own, lies spread;
I view that oak, the fancied glades among,
By which as Milton lay, his evening ear,
From many a cloud that dropped ethereal dew,
Nigh sphered in Heaven its native strains could hear;
On which that ancient trump he reached was hung;
  Thither oft, his glory greeting,
  From Waller's myrtle shades retreating,
With many a vow from Hope's aspiring tongue,

stanza continues

My trembling feet his guiding steps pursue;
  In vain—such bliss to one alone,
  Of all the sons of soul was known,
  And Heaven, and Fancy, kindred powers,
  Have now o'erturned the inspiring bowers,
Or curtained close such scene from every future view.

The Castaway

Obscurest night involved the sky,
  The Atlantic billows roared,
When such a destined wretch as I,
  Washed headlong from on board,
Of friends, of hope, of all bereft,
His floating home forever left.

No braver chief could Albion boast
  Than he with whom he went,
Nor ever ship left Albion's coast,
  With warmer wishes sent.
He loved them both, but both in vain,
Nor him beheld, nor her again.

Not long beneath the whelming brine,
  Expert to swim, he lay;
Nor soon he felt his strength decline,
  Or courage die away;
But waged with death a lasting strife,
Supported by despair of life.

He shouted; nor his friends had failed
  To check the vessel's course,
But so the furious blast prevailed,
  That, pitiless perforce,

stanza continues

They left their outcast mate behind,
And scudded still before the wind.

Some succor yet they could afford;
  And, such as storms allow,
The cask, the coop, the floated cord,
  Delayed not to bestow.
But he (they knew) nor ship, nor shore,
Whate'er they gave, should visit more.

Nor, cruel as it seemed, could he
  Their haste himself condemn,
Aware that flight, in such a sea,
  Alone could rescue them;
Yet bitter felt it still to die
Deserted, and his friends so nigh.

He long survives, who lives an hour
  In ocean, self-upheld;
And so long he, with unspent power,
  His destiny repelled;
And ever, as the minutes flew,
Entreated help, or cried, "Adieu!"

At length, his transient respite past,
  His comrades, who before

stanza continues

Had heard his voice in every blast,
  Could catch the sound no more.
For then, by toil subdued, he drank
The stifling wave, and then he sank.

No poet wept him; but the page
  Of narrative sincere,
That tells his name, his worth, his age,
  Is wet with Anson's tear.
And tears by bards or heroes shed
Alike immortalize the dead.

I therefore purpose not, or dream,
  Descanting on his fate,
To give the melancholy theme
  A more enduring date:
But misery still delights to trace
Its semblance in another's case.

No voice divine the storm allayed,
  No light propitious shone,
When, snatched from all effectual aid,
  We perished, each alone;
But I beneath a rougher sea,
And whelmed in deeper gulfs than he.

An Hymn to the Morning

Attend my lays, ye ever honour'd nine,
Assist my labours, and my strains refine;
In smoothest numbers pour the notes along,
For bright *Aurora* now demands my song.
  Aurora hail, and all the thousand dyes,
Which deck thy progress through the vaulted skies;
The morn awakes, and wide extends her rays,
On ev'ry leaf the gentle zephyr plays;
Harmonious lays the feather'd race resume,
Dart the bright eye, and shake the painted plume.
  Ye shady groves, your verdant gloom display
To shield your poet from the burning day:
Calliope awake the sacred lyre,
While thy fair sisters fan the pleasing fire:
The bow'rs, the gales, the variegated skies
In all their pleasures in my bosom rise.
  See in the east th' illustrious king of day!
His rising radiance drives the shades away—
But oh! I feel his fervid beams too strong,
And scarce begun, concludes th' abortive song.

To a Lady on the Death of Her Husband

Grim monarch! see, deprived of vital breath
A young physician in the dust of death!
Dost thou go on incessant to destroy?
The grief to double and lay waste the joy?
Enough thou never yet wast known to say,
Tho' millions die the vassals of thy sway:
Nor youth, nor science, nor the ties of love,
Nor aught on earth thy flinty heart can move.
The friend, the spouse, from his dire dart to save,
In vain we ask the sovereign of the grave.
Fair mourner, there see thy lov'd *Leonard* laid,
And o'er him spread the deep impervious shade;
Clos'd are his eyes and heavy fetters keep
His senses bound in never-waking sleep,
Till time shall cease, till many a starry world,
Shall fall from heav'n, in dire confusion hurl'd;
Till Nature in her final wreck shall lie,
Till Her last groan shall rend the azure sky;
Not till then his active soul shall claim,
His body, a divine immortal frame.
  But, see the softly stealing tears apace,
Pursue each other down the mourner's face;

stanza continues

But cease thy tears, bid ev'ry sigh depart,
And cast the load of anguish from thine heart;
From the cold shell of his great soul arise,
And look beyond, thou native of the skies;
There fix thy view where fleeter than the wind
Thy *Leonard* mounts, and leaves the earth behind.

Thyself prepare to pass the vale of night,
To join forever on the hills of light;
To thine embrace, his joyful spirit moves,
To thee, the partner of his earthly loves;
He welcomes thee to pleasures more refin'd
And better suited to th' immortal mind.

A Poison Tree

I was angry with my friend;
I told my wrath—my wrath did end.
I was angry with my foe;
I told it not—my wrath did grow.

And I watered it in fears,
Night and morning with my tears,
And I sunned it with smiles,
And with soft deceitful wiles.

And it grew both day and night,
Till it bore an apple bright.
And my foe beheld it shine,
And he knew that it was mine,

And into my garden stole
When the night had veiled the pole.
In the morning glad I see
My foe outstretched beneath the tree.

A Vision of Albion

I see the Fourfold Man; the Humanity in
  deadly sleep,
And its fallen Emanation, the Spectre and its
  cruel Shadow.
I see the Past, Present, and Future existing all
  at once
Before me. O Divine Spirit! sustain me on thy
  wings,
That I may awake Albion from his long and
  cold repose;
For Bacon and Newton, sheath'd in dismal steel,
  their terrors hang
Like iron scourges over Albion. Reasonings like
  vast Serpents
Enfold around my limbs, bruising my minute
  articulations.
I turn my eyes to the Schools and Universities
  of Europe,
And there behold the Loom of Locke, whose
  Woof rages dire,
Wash'd by the Water-wheels of Newton: black
  the cloth
In heavy wreaths folds over every Nation:
  cruel Works

continues

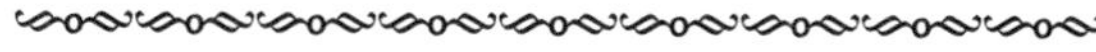

Of many Wheels I view, wheel without wheel, with cogs tyrannic,
Moving by compulsion each other; not as those in Eden, which,
Wheel within wheel, in freedom revolve, in harmony and peace.

A Vision of Eternity

Eternity appear'd above them as One Man, enfolded
In Luvah's robes of blood, and bearing all his
afflictions:
As the sun shines down on the misty earth, such
was the Vision.
But purple Night, and crimson Morning, and
golden Day, descending
Thro' the clear changing atmosphere, display'd
green fields among
The varying clouds, like Paradises stretch'd in the
expanse,
With towns, and villages, and temples, tents, sheep-
folds and pastures,
Where dwell the children of the Elemental worlds
in harmony.

Ah! Sunflower

Ah! sunflower, weary of time,
Who countest the steps of the sun,
Seeking after that sweet golden clime
Where the traveller's journey is done;

Where the youth pined away with desire,
And the pale virgin shrouded in snow,
Arise from their graves and aspire;
Where my sunflower wishes to go.

Auguries of Innocence

To see a World in a grain of sand,
And a Heaven in a wild flower,
Hold Infinity in the palm of your hand,
And Eternity in an hour.
A robin redbreast in a cage
Puts all Heaven in a rage.
A dove-house fill'd with doves and pigeons
Shudders Hell thro' all its regions.
A dog starv'd at his master's gate
Predicts the ruin of the State.
A horse misus'd upon the road
Calls to Heaven for human blood.
Each outcry of the hunted hare
A fibre from the brain does tear.
A skylark wounded in the wing,
A cherubim does cease to sing.
The game-cock clipt and arm'd for fight
Does the rising sun affright.
Every wolf's and lion's howl
Raises from Hell a Human soul.
The wild deer, wandering here and there,
Keeps the Human soul from care.
The lamb misus'd breeds public strife,
And yet forgives the butcher's knife.

continues

The bat that flits at close of eve
Has left the brain that won't believe.
The owl that calls upon the night
Speaks the unbeliever's fright.
He who shall hurt the little wren
Shall never be belov'd by men.
He who the ox to wrath has mov'd
Shall never be by woman lov'd.
The wanton boy that kills the fly
Shall feel the spider's enmity.
He who torments the chafer's sprite
Weaves a bower in endless night.
The caterpillar on the leaf
Repeats to thee thy mother's grief.
Kill not the moth nor butterfly,
For the Last Judgement draweth nigh.
He who shall train the horse to war
Shall never pass the polar bar.
The beggar's dog and widow's cat,
Feed them, and thou wilt grow fat.
The gnat that sings his summer's song
Poison gets from Slander's tongue.
The poison of the snake and newt
Is the sweat of Envy's foot.
The poison of the honey-bee
Is the artist's jealousy.
The prince's robes and beggar's rags
Are toadstools on the miser's bags.

A truth that's told with bad intent
Beats all the lies you can invent.
It is right it should be so;
Man was made for joy and woe;
And when this we rightly know,
Thro' the world we safely go.
Joy and woe are woven fine,
A clothing for the soul divine;
Under every grief and pine
Runs a joy with silken twine.
The babe is more than swaddling-bands;
Throughout all these human lands
Tools were made, and born were hands,
Every farmer understands.
Every tear from every eye
Becomes a babe in Eternity;
This is caught by Females bright,
And return'd to its own delight.
The bleat, the bark, bellow, and roar
Are waves that beat on Heaven's shore.
The babe that weeps the rod beneath
Writes revenge in realms of death.
The beggar's rags, fluttering in air,
Does to rags the heaven's tear.
The soldier, arm'd with sword and gun,
Palsied strikes the summer's sun.

continues

The poor man's farthing is worth more
Than all the gold on Afric's shore.
One mite wrung from the labourer's hands
Shall buy and sell the miser's lands
Or, if protected from on high,
Does that whole nation sell and buy.
He who mocks the infant's faith
Shall be mock'd in Age and Death.
He who shall teach the child to doubt
The rotting grave shall ne'er get out.
He who respects the infant's faith
Triumphs over Hell and Death.
The child's toys and the old man's reasons
Are the fruits of the two seasons.
The questioner, who sits so sly,
Shall never know how to reply.
He who replies to words of Doubt
Doth put the light of knowledge out.
The strongest poison ever known
Came from Caesar's laurel crown.
Nought can deform the human race
Like to the armour's iron brace.
When gold and gems adorn the plough
To peaceful arts shall Envy bow.
A riddle, or the cricket's cry,
Is to Doubt a fit reply.
The emmet's inch and eagle's mile
Make lame Philosophy to smile.

He who doubts from what he sees
Will ne'er believe, do what you please.
If the Sun and Moon should doubt,
They'd immediately go out.
To be in a passion you good may do,
But no good if a passion is in you.
The whore and gambler, by the state
Licensed, build that nation's fate.
The harlot's cry from street to street
Shall weave Old England's winding-sheet.
The winner's shout, the loser's curse,
Dance before dead England's hearse.
Every night and every morn
Some to misery are born.
Every morn and every night
Some are born to sweet delight.
Some are born to sweet delight,
Some are born to endless night.
We are led to believe a lie
When we see not thro' the eye,
Which was born in a night, to perish in a night,
When the Soul slept in beams of light.
God appears, and God is Light,
To those poor souls who dwell in Night;
But does a Human Form display
To those who dwell in realms of Day.

London

I wander thro' each charter'd street,
Near where the charter'd Thames does flow,
And mark in every face I meet
Marks of weakness, marks of woe.

In every cry of every Man,
In every Infant's cry of fear,
In every voice, in every ban,
The mind-forg'd manacles I hear.

How the chimney-sweeper's cry
Every black'ning church appals;
And the hapless soldier's sigh
Runs in blood down palace walls.

But most thro' midnight streets I hear
How the youthful harlot's curse
Blasts the new-born infant's tear,
And blights with plagues the marriage hearse.

The Tyger

Tyger, Tyger, burning bright,
In the forests of the night:
What immortal hand or eye
Could frame thy fearful symmetry?

In what distant deeps or skies,
Burnt the fire of thine eyes?
On what wings dare he aspire?
What the hand dare seize the fire?

And what shoulder, and what art,
Could twist the sinews of thy heart?
And when thy heart began to beat,
What dread hand? and what dread feet?

What the hammer? what the chain?
In what furnace was thy brain?
What the anvil? what dread grasp
Dare its deadly terrors clasp?

When the stars threw down their spears,
And watered Heaven with their tears,
Did he smile his work to see?
Did he who made the lamb make thee?

continues

Tyger, tyger, burning bright,
In the forests of the night:
What immortal hand or eye
Dare frame thy fearful symmetry?

For A' That and A' That

Is there, for honest poverty,
  That hangs his head, and a' that?
The coward slave, we pass him by,
  We dare be poor for a' that!
    For a' that, and a' that,
      Our toils obscure, and a' that;
    The rank is but the guinea's stamp,
      The man's the gowd for a' that.

What though on hamely fare we dine,
  Wear hodden-grey, and a' that?
Gie fools their silks, and knaves their wine,
  A man's a man for a' that;
    For a' that, and a' that,
      Their tinsel show, and a' that;
    The honest man, though e'er sae poor,
      Is king o' men for a' that.

Ye see yon birkie, ca'd a lord,
  Wha struts, and stares, and a' that!
Though hundreds worship at his word,
  He's but a coof for a' that:
    For a' that, and a' that,

stanza continues

His riband, star, and a' that,
The man of independent mind,
He looks and laughs at a' that.

A prince can mak a belted knight,
A marquis, duke, and a' that!
But an honest man's aboon his might,
Guid faith he mauna fa' that!
For a' that, and a' that,
Their dignities, and a' that,
The pith o' sense, and pride o' worth,
Are higher rank than a' that.

Then let us pray that come it may,
As come it will for a' that,
That sense and worth, o'er a' the earth,
May bear the gree, and a' that.
For a' that, and a' that,
It's coming yet, for a' that,
That man to man the warld o'er
Shall brothers be for a' that.

Ode on Intimations of Immortality

from *RECOLLECTIONS OF EARLY CHILDHOOD*

There was a time when meadow, grove, and stream,
The earth, and every common sight,
To me did seem
Apparelled in celestial light,
The glory and the freshness of a dream.
It is not now as it hath been of yore;—
Turn wheresoe'er I may,
By night or day,
The things which I have seen I now can see no more.
The rainbow comes and goes,
And lovely is the rose;
The moon doth with delight
Look round her when the heavens are bare;
Waters on a starry night
Are beautiful and fair;
The sunshine is a glorious birth;
But yet I know, where'er I go,
That there hath past away a glory from the earth.

Now, while the birds thus sing a joyous song,
And while the young lambs bound
As to the tabor's sound,

stanza continues

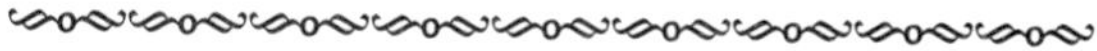

To me alone there came a thought of grief:
A timely utterance gave that thought relief;
    And I again am strong.
The cataracts blow their trumpets from the steep;—
Nor more shall grief of mine the season wrong:
I hear the echoes through the mountains throng,
The winds come to me from the fields of sleep,
    And all the earth is gay;
        Land and sea
    Give themselves up to jollity,
    And with the heart of May
    Doth every beast keep holiday;—
        Thou child of joy,
Shout round me, let me hear thy shouts, thou
  happy shepherd-boy!

Ye blessèd Creatures, I have heard the call
  Ye to each other make; I see
The heavens laugh with you in your jubilee;
  My heart is at your festival,
  My head hath its coronal,
The fullness of your bliss, I feel—I feel it all.
    Oh evil day! if I were sullen
    While Earth herself is adorning
        This sweet May-morning,
    And the children are culling

stanza continues

On every side,
In a thousand valleys far and wide,
Fresh flowers; while the sun shines warm
And the Babe leaps up on his mother's arm:—
I hear, I hear, with joy I hear!
—But there's a tree, of many, one,
A single field which I have looked upon,
Both of them speak of something that is gone:
The pansy at my feet
Doth the same tale repeat:
Whither is fled the visionary gleam?
Where is it now, the glory and the dream?

Our birth is but a sleep and a forgetting;
The Soul that rises with us, our life's Star,
Hath had elsewhere its setting
And cometh from afar;
Not in entire forgetfulness,
And not in utter nakedness,
But trailing clouds of glory do we come
From God, who is our home:
Heaven lies about us in our infancy!
Shades of the prison-house begin to close
Upon the growing Boy,
But he beholds the light, and whence it flows,
He sees it in his joy;

stanza continues

The Youth, who daily farther from the east
  Must travel, still is Nature's Priest,
    And by the vision splendid
  Is on his way attended;
At length the Man perceives it die away,
And fade into the light of common day.

Earth fills her lap with pleasures of her own;
Yearnings she hath in her own natural kind,
And, even with something of a Mother's mind,
      And no unworthy aim,
    The homely nurse doth all she can
To make her Foster-child, her inmate, Man,
      Forget the glories he hath known,
And the imperial palace whence he came.

Behold the Child among his new-born blisses,
A six years' darling of a pigmy size!
See, where 'mid work of his own hand he lies,
Fretted by sallies of his mother's kisses,
With light upon him from his father's eyes!
See, at his feet, some little plan or chart,
Some fragment from his dream of human life,
Shaped by himself with newly-learnèd art;
    A wedding or a festival,
    A mourning or a funeral;

stanza continues

And this hath now his heart,
And unto this he frames his song:
Then will he fit his tongue
To dialogues of business, love, or strife;
But it will not be long
Ere this be thrown aside,
And with new joy and pride
The little actor cons another part;
Filling from time to time his 'humorous stage'
With all the Persons, down to palsied Age,
That Life brings with her in her equipage;
As if his whole vocation
Were endless imitation.

Thou, whose exterior semblance doth belie
Thy soul's immensity;
Thou best philosopher, who yet dost keep
Thy heritage, thou eye among the blind,
That, deaf and silent, read'st the eternal deep,
Haunted for ever by the eternal mind, —
Mighty Prophet! Seer blest!
On whom those truths do rest
Which we are toiling all our lives to find,
In darkness lost, the darkness of the grave;
Thou, over whom thy Immortality
Broods like the day, a master o'er a slave,

stanza continues

A presence which is not to be put by;
Thou little child yet glorious in the might
Of heaven-born freedom on thy being's height,
Why with such earnest pains dost thou provoke
The years to bring the inevitable yoke,
Thus blindly with thy blessedness at strife?
Full soon thy Soul shall have her earthly freight,
And custom lie upon thee with a weight,
Heavy as frost, and deep almost as life!

Oh joy! that in our embers
Is something that doth live,
That nature yet remembers
What was so fugitive!
The thought of our past years in me doth breed
Perpetual benediction: not indeed
For that which is most worthy to be blest;
Delight and liberty, the simple creed
Of Childhood, whether busy or at rest,
With new-fledged hope still fluttering in his
breast:—
Not for these I raise
The song of thanks and praise;
But for those obstinate questionings
Of sense and outward things,
Fallings from us, vanishings;
Blank misgivings of a creature

stanza continues

Moving about in worlds not realized,
High instincts before which our mortal nature
Did tremble like a guilty thing surprised:
But for those first affections,
Those shadowy recollections,
Which, be they what they may,
Are yet the fountain-light of all our day,
Are yet a master-light of all our seeing;
Uphold us, cherish, and have power to make
Our noisy years seem moments in the being
Of the eternal Silence: truths that wake,
To perish never;
Which neither listlessness, nor mad endeavour,
Nor man nor boy,
Nor all that is at enmity with joy,
Can utterly abolish or destroy!
Hence in a season of calm weather,
Though inland far we be,
Our Souls have sight of that immortal sea
Which brought us hither,
Can in a moment travel thither,
And see the children sport upon the shore,
And hear the mighty waters rolling evermore.

Then sing, ye birds, sing, sing a joyous song!
And let the young Lambs bound
As to the tabor's sound!

stanza continues

We in thought will join your throng
  Ye that pipe and ye that play,
  Ye that through your hearts today
  Feel the gladness of the May!
What though the radiance which was once so bright
Be now for ever taken from my sight,
  Though nothing can bring back the hour
Of splendour in the grass, of glory in the flower;
    We will grieve not, rather find
    Strength in what remains behind;
    In the primal sympathy
    Which having been must ever be;
    In the soothing thoughts that spring
    Out of human suffering;
    In the faith that looks through death,
In years that bring the philosophic mind.

And O, ye Fountains, Meadows, Hills, and Groves,
Forbode not any severing of our loves!
Yet in my heart of hearts I feel your might;
I only have relinquished one delight
To live beneath your more habitual sway:
I love the brooks which down their channels fret,
Even more than when I tripped lightly as they;
The innocent brightness of a new-born day
      Is lovely yet;

stanza continues

The clouds that gather round the setting sun
Do take a sober colouring from an eye
That hath kept watch o'er man's mortality;
Another race hath been, and other palms are won.
Thanks to the human heart by which we live,
Thanks to its tenderness, its joys, and fears,
To me the meanest flower that blows can give
Thoughts that do often lie too deep for tears.

The World Is Too Much with Us

The world is too much with us; late and soon,
Getting and spending, we lay waste our powers;
Little we see in Nature that is ours;
We have given our hearts away, a sordid boon!
This Sea that bares her bosom to the moon,
The winds that will be howling at all hours,
And are up-gathered now like sleeping flowers,
For this, for everything, we are out of tune;
It moves us not.—Great God! I'd rather be
A Pagan suckled in a creed outworn;
So might I, standing on this pleasant lea,
Have glimpses that would make me less forlorn;
Have sight of Proteus rising from the sea;
Or hear old Triton blow his wreathèd horn.

Kubla Khan: Or a Vision in a Dream. A Fragment

In Xanadu did Kubla Khan
A stately pleasure dome decree:
Where Alph, the sacred river, ran
Through caverns measureless to man
   Down to a sunless sea.
So twice five miles of fertile ground
With walls and towers were girdled round:
And there were gardens bright with sinuous rills,
Where blossomed many an incense-bearing tree;
And here were forests ancient as the hills,
Enfolding sunny spots of greenery.

But oh! that deep romantic chasm which slanted
Down the green hill athwart a cedarn cover!
A savage place! as holy and enchanted
As e'er beneath a waning moon was haunted
By woman wailing for her demon lover!
And from this chasm, with ceaseless turmoil seething,
As if this earth in fast thick pants were breathing,
A mighty fountain momently was forced:
Amid whose swift half-intermitted burst
Huge fragments vaulted like rebounding hail,
Or chaffy grain beneath the thresher's flail:

stanza continues

And 'mid these dancing rocks at once and ever
It flung up momently the sacred river.
Five miles meandering with a mazy motion
Through wood and dale the sacred river ran,
Then reached the caverns measureless to man,
And sank in tumult to a lifeless ocean:
And 'mid this tumult Kubla heard from far
Ancestral voices prophesying war!

The shadow of the dome of pleasure
Floated midway on the waves;
Where was heard the mingled measure
From the fountain and the caves.
It was a miracle of rare device,
A sunny pleasure dome with caves of ice!

A damsel with a dulcimer
In a vision once I saw:
It was an Abyssinian maid,
And on her dulcimer she played,
Singing of Mount Abora.
Could I revive within me
Her symphony and song,
To such a deep delight 'twould win me,
That with music loud and long,
I would build that dome in air,
That sunny dome! those caves of ice!

stanza continues

And all who heard should see them there,
And all should cry, Beware! Beware!
His flashing eyes, his floating hair!
Weave a circle round him thrice,
And close your eyes with holy dread,
For he on honey-dew hath fed,
And drunk the milk of Paradise.

from The Rime of the Ancient Mariner

Part I

It is an ancient Mariner
And he stoppeth one of three.
—"By thy long gray beard and glittering eye,
Now wherefore stopp'st thou me?

The Bridegroom's doors are opened wide,
And I am next of kin;
The guests are met, the feast is set:
May'st hear the merry din."

He holds him with his skinny hand,
"There was a ship," quoth he.
"Hold off! unhand me, graybeard loon!"
Eftsoons his hand dropped he.

He holds him with his glittering eye—
The Wedding Guest stood still,
And listens like a three years' child:
The Mariner hath his will.

The Wedding Guest sat on a stone:
He cannot choose but hear;
And thus spake on that ancient man,
The bright-eyed Mariner.

"The ship was cheered, the harbor cleared,
Merrily did we drop
Below the kirk, below the hill,
Below the lighthouse top.

The Sun came up upon the left,
Out of the sea came he!
And he shone bright, and on the right
Went down into the sea.

Higher and higher every day,
Till over the mast at noon—"
The Wedding Guest here beat his breast,
For he heard the loud bassoon.

The bride hath paced into the hall,
Red as a rose is she;
Nodding their heads before her goes
The merry minstrelsy.

The Wedding Guest he beat his breast,
Yet he cannot choose but hear;
And thus spake on that ancient man,
The bright-eyed Mariner.

"And now the STORM-BLAST came, and he
Was tyrannous and strong;
He struck with his o'ertaking wings,
And chased us south along.

continues

With sloping masts and dipping prow,
As who pursued with yell and blow
Still treads the shadow of his foe,
And forward bends his head,
The ship drove fast, loud roared the blast,
And southward aye we fled.

And now there came both mist and snow,
And it grew wondrous cold:
And ice, mast-high, came floating by,
As green as emerald.

And through the drifts the snowy clifts
Did send a dismal sheen:
Nor shapes of men nor beasts we ken—
The ice was all between.

The ice was here, the ice was there,
The ice was all around:
It cracked and growled, and roared and howled,
Like noises in a swound!

At length did cross an Albatross,
Thorough the fog it came;
As if it had been a Christian soul,
We hailed it in God's name.

It ate the food it ne'er had eat,
And round and round it flew.
The ice did split with a thunder-fit;
The helmsman steered us through!

And a good south wind sprung up behind;
The Albatross did follow,
And every day, for food or play,
Came to the mariners' hollo!

In mist or cloud, on mast or shroud,
It perched for vespers nine;
Whiles all the night, through fog-smoke white,
Glimmered the white Moon-shine."

"God save thee, ancient Mariner!
From the fiends, that plague thee thus!—
Why look'st thou so?"—With my crossbow
I shot the ALBATROSS.

Part II

The Sun now rose upon the right:
Out of the sea came he,
Still hid in mist, and on the left
Went down into the sea.

continues

And the good south wind still blew behind,
But no sweet bird did follow,
Nor any day for food or play
Came to the mariners' hollo!

And I had done a hellish thing,
And it would work 'em woe:
For all averred, I had killed the bird
That made the breeze to blow.
Ah wretch! said they, the bird to slay,
That made the breeze to blow!

Nor dim nor red, like God's own head,
The glorious Sun uprist:
Then all averred, I had killed the bird
That brought the fog and mist.
'Twas right, said they, such birds to slay,
That bring the fog and mist.

The fair breeze blew, the white foam flew,
The furrow followed free;
We were the first that ever burst
Into that silent sea.

Down dropped the breeze, the sails dropped down,
'Twas sad as sad could be;
And we did speak only to break
The silence of the sea!

All in a hot and copper sky,
The bloody Sun, at noon,
Right up above the mast did stand,
No bigger than the Moon.

Day after day, day after day,
We stuck, nor breath nor motion;
As idle as a painted ship
Upon a painted ocean.

Water, water, everywhere,
And all the boards did shrink;
Water, water, everywhere,
Nor any drop to drink.

The very deep did rot: O Christ!
That ever this should be!
Yea, slimy things did crawl with legs
Upon the slimy sea.

About, about, in reel and rout
The death-fires danced at night;
The water, like a witch's oils,
Burnt green, and blue and white.

And some in dreams assuréd were
Of the Spirit that plagued us so;
Nine fathom deep he had followed us
From the land of mist and snow.

continues

And every tongue, through utter drought,
Was withered at the root;
We could not speak, no more than if
We had been choked with soot.

Ah! well-a-day! what evil looks
Had I from old and young!
Instead of the cross, the Albatross
About my neck was hung.

Part III

There passed a weary time. Each throat
Was parched, and glazed each eye.
A weary time! a weary time!
How glazed each weary eye,
When looking westward, I beheld
A something in the sky.

At first it seemed a little speck,
And then it seemed a mist;
It moved and moved, and took at last
A certain shape, I wist.

A speck, a mist, a shape, I wist!
And still it neared and neared:
As if it dodged a water sprite,
It plunged and tacked and veered.

With throats unslaked, with black lips baked,
We could nor laugh nor wail;
Through utter drought all dumb we stood!
I bit my arm, I sucked the blood,
And cried, A sail! a sail!

With throats unslaked, with black lips baked,
Agape they heard me call:
Gramercy! they for joy did grin,
And all at once their breath drew in,
As they were drinking all.

See! see! (I cried) she tacks no more!
Hither to work us weal;
Without a breeze, without a tide,
She steadies with upright keel!

The western wave was all aflame.
The day was well nigh done!
Almost upon the western wave
Rested the broad bright Sun;
When that strange shape drove suddenly
Betwixt us and the Sun.

And straight the Sun was flecked with bars,
(Heaven's Mother send us grace!)
As if through a dungeon grate he peered
With broad and burning face.

continues

Alas! (thought I, and my heart beat loud)
How fast she nears and nears!
Are those *her* sails that glance in the Sun,
Like restless gossameres?

Are those *her* ribs through which the Sun
Did peer, as through a grate?
And is that Woman all her crew?
Is that a DEATH? and are there two?
Is DEATH that woman's mate?

Her lips were red, *her* looks were free,
Her locks were yellow as gold:
Her skin was as white as leprosy,
The Nightmare LIFE-IN-DEATH was she,
Who thicks man's blood with cold.

The naked hulk alongside came,
And the twain were casting dice;
"The game is done! I've won! I've won!"
Quoth she, and whistles thrice.

The Sun's rim dips; the stars rush out:
At one stride comes the dark;
With far-heard whisper, o'er the sea,
Off shot the specter-bark.

We listened and looked sideways up!
Fear at my heart, as at a cup,
My lifeblood seemed to sip!
The stars were dim, and thick the night,
The steersman's face by his lamp gleamed white;
From the sails the dew did drip—
Till clomb above the eastern bar
The hornéd Moon, with one bright star
Within the nether tip.

One after one, by the star-dogged Moon,
Too quick for groan or sigh,
Each turned his face with ghastly pang,
And cursed me with his eye.

Four times fifty living men,
(And I heard nor sigh nor groan)
With heavy thump, a lifeless lump,
They dropped down one by one.

The souls did from their bodies fly—
They fled to bliss or woe!
And every soul, it passed me by,
Like the whizz of my cross-bow!

continues

Part IV

"I fear thee, ancient Mariner!
I fear thy skinny hand!
And thou art long, and lank, and brown,
As is the ribbed sea-sand.

I fear thee and thy glittering eye,
And thy skinny hand, so brown."—
Fear not, fear not, thou Wedding Guest!
This body dropped not down.

Alone, alone, all, all alone,
Alone on a wide wide sea!
And never a saint took pity on
My soul in agony.

The many men, so beautiful!
And they all dead did lie:
And a thousand thousand slimy things
Lived on; and so did I.

I looked upon the rotting sea,
And drew my eyes away;
I looked upon the rotting deck,
And there the dead men lay.

I looked to heaven, and tried to pray;
But or ever a prayer had gushed,
A wicked whisper came, and made
My heart as dry as dust.

I closed my lids, and kept them close,
And the balls like pulses beat,
For the sky and the sea, and the sea and the sky
Lay like a load on my weary eye,
And the dead were at my feet.

The cold sweat melted from their limbs,
Nor rot nor reek did they:
The look with which they looked on me
Had never passed away.

An orphan's curse would drag to hell
A spirit from on high;
But oh! more horrible than that
Is the curse in a dead man's eye!
Seven days, seven nights, I saw that curse,
And yet I could not die.

The moving Moon went up the sky,
And nowhere did abide:
Softly she was going up,
And a star or two beside—

continues

Her beams bemocked the sultry main,
Like April hoar-frost spread;
But where the ship's huge shadow lay,
The charméd water burnt alway
A still and awful red.

Beyond the shadow of the ship,
I watched the water snakes:
They moved in tracks of shining white,
And when they reared, the elfish light
Fell off in hoary flakes.

Within the shadow of the ship
I watched their rich attire:
Blue, glossy green, and velvet black,
They coiled and swam; and every track
Was a flash of golden fire.

O happy living things! no tongue
Their beauty might declare:
A spring of love gushed from my heart,
And I blessed them unaware:
Sure my kind saint took pity on me,
And I blessed them unaware.

The self-same moment I could pray;
And from my neck so free
The Albatross fell off, and sank
Like lead into the sea.

Prometheus

Titan! to whose immortal eyes
  The sufferings of mortality,
  Seen in their sad reality,
Were not as things that gods despise;
What was thy pity's recompense?
A silent suffering, and intense;
The rock, the vulture, and the chain,
All that the proud can feel of pain,
The agony they do not show,
The suffocating sense of woe,
  Which speaks but in its loneliness,
And then is jealous lest the sky
Should have a listener, nor will sigh
  Until its voice is echoless.

Titan! to thee the strife was given
  Between the suffering and the will,
  Which torture where they cannot kill;
And the inexorable Heaven,
And the deaf tyranny of Fate,
The ruling principle of Hate,
Which for its pleasure doth create
The things it may annihilate,
Refused thee even the boon to die:

stanza continues

LORD BYRON (1788–1824)

The wretched gift eternity
Was thine—and thou hast borne it well.
All that the Thunderer wrung from thee
Was but the menace which flung back
On him the torments of thy rack;
The fate thou didst so well foresee,
But would not to appease him tell;
And in thy Silence was his Sentence,
And in his Soul a vain repentance,
And evil dread so ill dissembled,
That in his hand the lightnings trembled.

Thy Godlike crime was to be kind,
  To render with thy precepts less
  The sum of human wretchedness,
And strengthen Man with his own mind;
But baffled as thou wert from high,
Still in thy patient energy,
In the endurance, and repulse
  Of thine impenetrable Spirit,
Which Earth and Heaven could not convulse,
  A mighty lesson we inherit:
Thou art a symbol and a sign
  To Mortals of their fate and force;
Like thee, Man is in part divine,
  A troubled stream from a pure source;

stanza continues

And Man in portions can foresee
His own funereal destiny,
His wretchedness, and his resistance,
And his sad unallied existence:
To which his Spirit may oppose
Itself—and equal to all woes,
  And a firm will, and a deep sense,
Which even in torture can descry
  Its own concenter'd recompense,
Triumphant where it dares defy,
And making Death a Victory.

Hymn to Intellectual Beauty

1

The awful shadow of some unseen Power
  Floats though unseen among us—visiting
  This various world with as inconstant wing
As summer winds that creep from flower to
    flower—
Like moonbeams that behind some piny mountain
    shower,
  It visits with inconstant glance
  Each human heart and countenance;
Like hues and harmonies of evening—
  Like clouds in starlight widely spread—
  Like memory of music fled—
  Like aught that for its grace may be
Dear, and yet dearer for its mystery.

2

Spirit of BEAUTY, that dost consecrate
  With thine own hues all thou dost shine upon
  Of human thought or form—where art thou gone?
Why dost thou pass away and leave our state,
This dim vast vale of tears, vacant and desolate?
  Ask why the sunlight not forever
  Weaves rainbows o'er yon mountain river,

stanza continues

Why aught should fail and fade that once is shown,
Why fear and dream and death and birth
Cast on the daylight of this earth
Such gloom—why man has such a scope
For love and hate, despondency and hope?

3

No voice from some sublimer world hath ever
To sage or poet these responses given—
Therefore the names of Daemon, Ghost, and
Heaven,
Remain the records of their vain endeavor,
Frail spells—whose uttered charm might not avail
to sever,
From all we hear and all we see,
Doubt, chance, and mutability.
Thy light alone—like mist o'er mountains driven,
Or music by the night wind sent
Through strings of some still instrument,
Or moonlight on a midnight stream,
Gives grace and truth to life's unquiet dream.

4

Love, Hope, and Self-esteem, like clouds depart
And come, for some uncertain moments lent.
Man were immortal, and omnipotent,

stanza continues

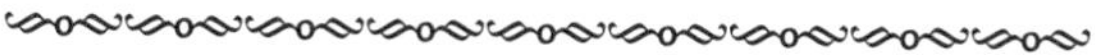

Didst thou, unknown and awful as thou art,
Keep with thy glorious train firm state within
his heart.
Thou messenger of sympathies,
That wax and wane in lovers' eyes—
Thou—that to human thought art nourishment,
Like darkness to a dying flame!
Depart not as thy shadow came,
Depart not—lest the grave should be,
Like life and fear, a dark reality.

5

While yet a boy I sought for ghosts, and sped
Through many a listening chamber, cave and ruin,
And starlight wood, with fearful steps pursuing
Hopes of high talk with the departed dead.
I called on poisonous names with which our youth
is fed;
I was not heard—I saw them not—
When musing deeply on the lot
Of life, at that sweet time when winds are wooing
All vital things that wake to bring
News of birds and blossoming—
Sudden, thy shadow fell on me;
I shrieked, and clasped my hands in ecstasy!

6

I vowed that I would dedicate my powers
To thee and thine—have I not kept the vow?
With beating heart and streaming eyes, even now
I call the phantoms of a thousand hours
Each from his voiceless grave: they have in visioned bowers
Of studious zeal or love's delight
Outwatched with me the envious night—
They know that never joy illumed my brow
Unlinked with hope that thou wouldst free
This world from its dark slavery,
That thou—O awful LOVELINESS,
Wouldst give whate'er these words cannot express.

7

The day becomes more solemn and serene
When noon is past—there is a harmony
In autumn, and a luster in its sky,
Which through the summer is not heard or seen,
As if it could not be, as if it had not been!
Thus let thy power, which like the truth
Of nature on my passive youth
Descended, to my onward life supply
Its calm—to one who worships thee,
And every form containing thee,
Whom, SPIRIT fair, thy spells did bind
To fear himself, and love all human kind.

To a Skylark

Hail to thee, blithe Spirit!
  Bird thou never wert,
That from Heaven, or near it,
  Pourest thy full heart
In profuse strains of unpremeditated art.

Higher still and higher
  From the earth thou springest
Like a cloud of fire;
  The blue deep thou wingest,
And singing still dost soar, and soaring ever singest.

In the golden lightning
  Of the sunken sun,
O'er which clouds are bright'ning,
  Thou dost float and run;
Like an unbodied joy whose race is just begun.

The pale purple even
  Melts around thy flight;
Like a star of Heaven,
  In the broad daylight
Thou art unseen, but yet I hear thy shrill delight,

Keen as are the arrows
  Of that silver sphere,
Whose intense lamp narrows
  In the white dawn clear
Until we hardly see—we feel that it is there.

All the earth and air
  With thy voice is loud,
As, when night is bare,
  From one lonely cloud
The moon rains out her beams, and Heaven is
  overflowed.

What thou art we know not;
  What is most like thee?
From rainbow clouds there flow not
  Drops so bright to see
As from thy presence showers a rain of melody.

Like a Poet hidden
  In the light of thought,
Singing hymns unbidden,
  Till the world is wrought
To sympathy with hopes and fears it heeded not:

continues

Like a high-born maiden
  In a palace tower,
Soothing her love-laden
  Soul in secret hour
With music sweet as love, which overflows
  her bower:

Like a glowworm golden
  In a dell of dew,
Scattering unbeholden
  Its aërial hue
Among the flowers and grass, which screen it
  from the view!

Like a rose embowered
  In its own green leaves,
By warm winds deflowered,
  Till the scent it gives
Makes faint with too much sweet those heavy-
  wingéd thieves:

Sound of vernal showers
  On the twinkling grass,
Rain-awakened flowers,
  All that ever was
Joyous, and clear, and fresh, thy music doth
  surpass:

Teach us, Sprite or Bird,
  What sweet thoughts are thine:
I have never heard
  Praise of love or wine
That panted forth a flood of rapture so divine.

Chorus Hymeneal,
  Or triumphal chant,
Matched with thine would be all
  But an empty vaunt,
A thing wherein we feel there is some hidden want.

What objects are the fountains
  Of thy happy strain?
What fields, or waves, or mountains?
  What shapes of sky or plain?
What love of thine own kind? what ignorance
  of pain?

With thy clear keen joyance
  Languor cannot be:
Shadow of annoyance
  Never came near thee:
Thou lovest—but ne'er knew love's sad satiety.

continues

Waking or asleep,
  Thou of death must deem
Things more true and deep
  Than we mortals dream,
Or how could thy notes flow in such a crystal stream?

We look before and after,
  And pine for what is not:
Our sincerest laughter
  With some pain is fraught;
Our sweetest songs are those that tell of saddest
  thought.

Yet if we could scorn
  Hate, and pride, and fear;
If we were things born
  Not to shed a tear,
I know not how thy joy we ever should come near.

Better than all measures
  Of delightful sound,
Better than all treasures
  That in books are found,
Thy skill to poet were, thou scorner of the ground!

Teach me half the gladness
  That thy brain must know,
Such harmonious madness
  From my lips would flow
The world should listen then—as I am listening now.

When I Have Fears

When I have fears that I may cease to be
  Before my pen has gleaned my teeming brain,
Before high-pilèd books, in charact'ry,
  Hold like rich garners the full-ripened grain;
When I behold, upon the night's starred face,
  Huge cloudy symbols of a high romance,
And think that I may never live to trace
  Their shadows, with the magic hand of chance;
And when I feel, fair creature of an hour,
  That I shall never look upon thee more,
Never have relish in the faery power
  Of unreflecting love!—then on the shore
Of the wide world I stand alone, and think
Till Love and Fame to nothingness do sink.

Ode on a Grecian Urn

Thou still unravished bride of quietness,
  Thou foster child of Silence and slow Time,
Sylvan historian, who canst thus express
  A flowery tale more sweetly than our rhyme:
What leaf-fring'd legend haunts about thy shape
  Of deities or mortals, or of both,
    In Tempe or the dales of Arcady?
What men or gods are these? What maidens loath?
  What mad pursuit? What struggle to escape?
    What pipes and timbrels? What wild ecstasy?

Heard melodies are sweet, but those unheard
  Are sweeter; therefore, ye soft pipes, play on;
Not to the sensual ear, but more endeared,
  Pipe to the spirit ditties of no tone;
Fair youth, beneath the trees, thou canst not leave
  Thy song, nor ever can those trees be bare;
    Bold Lover, never, never canst thou kiss,
Though winning near the goal—yet, do not grieve;
  She cannot fade, though thou hast not thy bliss,
    For ever wilt thou love, and she be fair!

Ah, happy, happy boughs! that cannot shed
  Your leaves, nor ever bid the Spring adieu;

stanza continues

And, happy melodist, unweariéd,
  For ever piping songs for ever new;
More happy love! more happy, happy love!
  For ever warm and still to be enjoy'd,
    For ever panting, and for ever young;
All breathing human passion far above,
  That leaves a heart high-sorrowful and cloy'd,
    A burning forehead, and a parching tongue.

Who are these coming to the sacrifice?
  To what green altar, O mysterious priest,
Lead'st thou that heifer lowing at the skies,
  And all her silken flanks with garlands drest?
What little town by river or seashore,
  Or mountain-built with peaceful citadel,
    Is emptied of this folk, this pious morn?
And, little town, thy streets for evermore
  Will silent be; and not a soul to tell
    Why thou are desolate, can e'er return.

O Attic shape! Fair attitude! with brede
  Of marble men and maidens overwrought,
With forest branches and the trodden weed;
  Thou, silent form, dost tease us out of thought
As doth eternity: Cold Pastoral!

stanza continues

When old age shall this generation waste,
Thou shalt remain, in midst of other woe
Than ours, a friend to man, to whom thou say'st,
"Beauty is truth, truth beauty,"—that is all
Ye know on earth, and all ye need to know.

Ode to a Nightingale

1

My heart aches, and a drowsy numbness pains
  My sense, as though of hemlock I had drunk,
Or emptied some dull opiate to the drains
  One minute past, and Lethe-wards had sunk:
'Tis not through envy of thy happy lot,
  But being too happy in thine happiness—
    That thou, light-wingéd Dryad of the trees,
        In some melodious plot
  Of beechen green, and shadows numberless,
    Singest of summer in full-throated ease.

2

O, for a draught of vintage! that hath been
  Cooled a long age in the deep-delvéd earth,
Tasting of Flora and the country green,
  Dance, and Provençal song, and sunburnt mirth!
O for a beaker full of the warm South,
  Full of the true, the blushful Hippocrene,
    With beaded bubbles winking at the brim,
        And purple-stainéd mouth;
  That I might drink, and leave the world unseen,
    And with thee fade away into the forest dim:

3

Fade far away, dissolve, and quite forget
  What thou among the leaves hast never known,
The weariness, the fever, and the fret
  Here, where men sit and hear each other groan;
Where palsy shakes a few, sad, last gray hairs,
  Where youth grows pale, and specter-thin,
    and dies,
   Where but to think is to be full of sorrow
      And leaden-eyed despairs,
  Where Beauty cannot keep her lustrous eyes,
   Or new Love pine at them beyond tomorrow.

4

Away! away! for I will fly to thee,
  Not charioted by Bacchus and his pards,
But on the viewless wings of Poesy,
  Though the dull brain perplexes and retards:
Already with thee! tender is the night,
  And haply the Queen-Moon is on her throne,
   Clustered around by all her starry Fays;
      But here there is no light,
  Save what from heaven is with the breezes blown
   Through verdurous glooms and winding
    mossy ways.

continues

5

I cannot see what flowers are at my feet,
  Nor what soft incense hangs upon the boughs,
But, in embalméd darkness, guess each sweet
  Wherewith the seasonable month endows
The grass, the thicket, and the fruit tree wild;
  White hawthorn, and the pastoral eglantine;
    Fast fading violets covered up in leaves;
        And mid-May's eldest child,
  The coming musk-rose, full of dewy wine,
    The murmurous haunt of flies on summer eves.

6

Darkling I listen; and for a many a time
  I have been half in love with easeful Death,
Called him soft names in many a muséd rhyme,
  To take into the air my quiet breath;
Now more than ever seems it rich to die,
  To cease upon the midnight with no pain,
    While thou art pouring forth thy soul abroad
        In such an ecstasy!
  Still wouldst thou sing, and I have ears in vain—
    To thy high requiem become a sod.

7

Thou wast not born for death, immortal Bird!
No hungry generations tread thee down;
The voice I hear this passing night was heard
In ancient days by emperor and clown:
Perhaps the selfsame song that found a path
Through the sad heart of Ruth, when, sick
for home,
She stood in tears amid the alien corn;
The same that ofttimes hath
Charmed magic casements, opening on the foam
Of perilous seas, in faery lands forlorn.

8

Forlorn! the very word is like a bell
To toll me back from thee to my sole self!
Adieu! the fancy cannot cheat so well
As she is famed to do, deceiving elf.
Adieu! adieu! thy plaintive anthem fades
Past the near meadows, over the still stream,
Up the hill side; and now 'tis buried deep
In the next valley-glades:
Was it a vision, or a waking dream?
Fled is that music:—Do I wake or sleep?

Days

Daughters of Time, the hypocritic Days,
Muffled and dumb like barefoot dervishes,
And marching single in an endless file,
Bring diadems and fagots in their hands.
To each they offer gifts after his will,
Bread, kingdoms, stars, and sky that holds them all.
I, in my pleached garden, watched the pomp,
Forgot my morning wishes, hastily
Took a few herbs and apples, and the Day
Turned and departed silent. I, too late,
Under her solemn fillet saw the scorn.

Earth Song

"Mine and yours;
Mine, not yours.
Earth endures;
Stars abide—
Shine down in the old sea;
Old are the shores;
But where are old men?
I who have seen much,
Such have I never seen.

"The lawyer's deed
Ran sure,
In tail,
To them, and to their heirs
Who shall succeed,
Without fail,
Forevermore.

"Here is the land,
Shaggy with wood,
With its old valley,
Mound and flood.
But the heritors?—
Fled like the flood's foam.

stanza continues

The lawyer, and the laws,
And the kingdom,
Clean swept herefrom.

"They called me theirs,
Who so controlled me;
Yet every one
Wished to stay, and is gone.
How am I theirs,
If they cannot hold me,
But I hold them?"

When I heard the Earth song
I was no longer brave;
My avarice cooled
Like lust in the chill of the grave.

Good-bye

Good-bye, proud world! I'm going home:
Thou art not my friend, and I'm not thine.
Long through thy weary crowds I roam;
A river ark on the ocean brine,
Long I've been tossed like the driven foam;
But now, proud world! I'm going home.

Good-bye to Flattery's fawning face;
To Grandeur with his wise grimace;
To upstart Wealth's averted eye;
So supple Office, low and high;
To crowded halls, to court and street;
To frozen hearts and hasting feet;
To those who go, and those who come;
Good-bye, proud world! I'm going home.

I am going to my own hearthstone,
Bosomed in yon green hills alone,—
A secret nook in a pleasant land,
Whose groves the frolic fairies planned;
Where arches green, the livelong day,
Echo the blackbird's roundelay,
And vulgar feet have never trod
A spot that is sacred to thought and God.

continues

O, when I am safe in my sylvan home
I tread on the pride of Greece and Rome;
And when I am stretched beneath the pines,
Where the evening star so holy shines,
I laugh at the lore and the pride of man,
At the sophist schools, and the learned clan;
For what are they all, in their high conceit
When man in the bush with God may meet?

The Day Is Done

The day is done, and the darkness
  Falls from the wings of Night,
As a feather is wafted downward
  From an eagle in his flight.

I see the lights of the village
  Gleam through the rain and the mist,
And a feeling of sadness comes o'er me
  That my soul cannot resist:

A feeling of sadness and longing,
  That is not akin to pain,
And resembles sorrow only
  As the mist resembles the rain.

Come, read to me some poem,
  Some simple and heartfelt lay,
That shall soothe this restless feeling,
  And banish the thoughts of day.

Not from the grand old masters
  Not from the bards sublime,
Whose distant footsteps echo
  Through the corridors of Time.

continues

For, like strains of martial music,
  Their mighty thoughts suggest
Life's endless toil and endeavor;
  And tonight I long for rest.

Read from some humbler poet,
  Whose songs gushed from his heart,
As showers from the clouds of summer,
  Or tears from the eyelids start;

Who, through long days of labor,
  And nights devoid of ease,
Still heard in his soul the music
  Of wonderful melodies.

Such songs have power to quiet
  The restless pulse of care,
And come like the benediction
  That follows after prayer.

Then read from the treasured volume
  The poem of thy choice,
And lend to the rhyme of the poet
  The beauty of thy voice.

And the night shall be filled with music
  And the cares, that infest the day,
Shall fold their tents, like the Arabs,
  And as silently steal away.

The Phantom Ship

In Mather's Magnalia Christi,
  Of the old colonial time,
May be found in prose the legend
  That is here set down in rhyme.

A ship sailed from New Haven,
  And the keen and frosty airs,
That filled her sails at parting,
  Were heavy with good men's prayers.

"O Lord! if it be thy pleasure"—
  Thus prayed the old divine—
"To bury our friends in the ocean,
  Take them, for they are thine!"

But Master Lamberton muttered,
  And under his breath said he,
"This ship is so crank and walty,
  I fear our grave she will be!"

And the ships that came from England,
  When the winter months were gone,
Brought no tidings of this vessel
  Nor of Master Lamberton

This put the people to praying
  That the Lord would let them hear
What in his greater wisdom
  He had done with friends so dear.

And at last their prayers were answered:
  It was in the month of June,
An hour before the sunset
  Of a windy afternoon,

When, steadily steering landward,
  A ship was seen below,
And they knew it was Lamberton, Master,
  Who sailed so long ago.

On she came, with a cloud of canvas,
  Right against the wind that blew
Until the eye could distinguish
  The faces of the crew.

Then fell her straining topmasts,
  Hanging tangled in the shrouds,
And her sails were loosened and lifted,
  And blown away like clouds.

continues

And the masts, with all their rigging,
  Fell slowly, one by one,
And the hulk dilated and vanished,
  As a sea-mist in the sun!

And the people who saw this marvel
  Each said unto his friend,
That this was the mould of their vessel,
  And thus her tragic end.

And the pastor of the village
  Gave thanks to God in prayer,
That, to quiet their troubled spirits,
  He had sent this Ship of Air.

Eldorado

Gaily bedight,
A gallant knight,
In sunshine and in shadow,
Had journeyed long,
Singing a song,
In search of Eldorado.

But he grew old—
This knight so bold—
And o'er his heart a shadow
Fell as he found
No spot of ground
That looked like Eldorado.

And, as his strength
Failed him at length,
He met a pilgrim shadow—
"Shadow," said he,
"Where can it be—
This land of Eldorado?"

"Over the Mountains
Of the Moon,
Down the Valley of the Shadow,

stanza continues

Ride, boldly ride,"
The shade replied,—
"If you seek for Eldorado!"

The Bells

Hear the sledges with the bells—
Silver bells!
What a world of merriment their melody foretells!
How they tinkle, tinkle, tinkle,
In the icy air of night!
While the stars that oversprinkle
All the heavens, seem to twinkle
With a crystalline delight;
Keeping time, time, time,
In a sort of Runic rhyme,
To the tintinnabulation that so musically wells
From the bells, bells, bells, bells,
Bells, bells, bells,—
From the jingling and the tinkling of the bells.

Hear the mellow wedding bells,
Golden bells!
What a world of happiness their harmony foretells!
Through the balmy air of night
How they ring out their delight!
From the molten-golden notes,
And all in tune,
What a liquid ditty floats
To the turtle dove that listens, while she gloats

stanza continues

On the moon!
Oh, from out the sounding cells,
What a gush of euphony voluminously wells!
How it swells!
How it dwells
On the Future! how it tells
Of the rapture that impels
To the swinging and the ringing
Of the bells, bells, bells,
Of the bells, bells, bells, bells,
Bells, bells, bells,—
To the rhyming and the chiming of the bells!

Hear the loud alarum bells—
Brazen bells!
What a tale of terror now their turbulency tells!
In the startled ear of night
How they scream out their affright!
Too much horrified to speak
They can only shriek, shriek,
Out of tune,
In a clamorous appealing to the mercy of the fire,
In a mad expostulation with the deaf and frantic fire,
Leaping higher, higher, higher,
With a desperate desire,
And a resolute endeavor,
Now—now to sit or never,

stanza continues

By the side of the pale-faced moon.
Oh, the bells, bells, bells!
What a tale their terror tells
Of despair!
How they clang, and clash, and roar!
What a horror they outpour
On the bosom of the palpitating air!
Yet the ear it fully knows,
By the twanging,
And the clanging,
How the danger ebbs and flows;
Yet the ear distinctly tells,
In the jangling,
And the wrangling,
How the danger sinks and swells,
By the sinking or the swelling in the anger of
the bells—
Of the bells—
Of the bells, bells, bells, bells,
Bells, bells, bells,—
In the clamor and the clangor of the bells!

Hear the tolling of the bells—
Iron bells!
What a world of solemn thought their monody
compels!

stanza continues

In the silence of the night,
How we shiver with affright
At the melancholy menace of their tone!
For every sound that floats
From the rust within their throats
        Is a groan.
And the people—ah, the people—
They that dwell up in the steeple,
        All alone,
And who tolling, tolling, tolling,
  In that muffled monotone,
Feel a glory in so rolling
  On the human heart a stone—
They are neither man nor woman—
They are neither brute nor human—
  They are Ghouls:
And their king it is who tolls;
And he rolls, rolls, rolls,
        Rolls
  A paean from the bells!
And his merry bosom swells
  With the paean of the bells!
And he dances, and he yells;
Keeping time, time, time,
In a sort of Runic rhyme,
  To the paean of the bells—
        Of the bells:

stanza continues

Keeping time, time, time,
In a sort of Runic rhyme,
To the throbbing of the bells—
Of the bells, bells, bells—
To the sobbing of the bells;
Keeping time, time, time,
As he knells, knells, knells,
In a happy Runic rhyme,
To the rolling of the bells—
Of the bells, bells, bells—
To the tolling of the bells,
Of the bells, bells, bells, bells—
Bells, bells, bells—
To the moaning and the groaning of the bells!

The Raven

Once upon a midnight dreary, while I pondered,
  weak and weary,
Over many a quaint and curious volume of forgotten
  lore—
While I nodded, nearly napping, suddenly there
  came a tapping,
As of some one gently rapping, rapping at my
  chamber door.
"'Tis some visiter," I muttered, "tapping at my
  chamber door—
        Only this and nothing more."

Ah, distinctly I remember it was in the bleak
  December;
And each separate dying ember wrought its ghost
  upon the floor.
Eagerly I wished the morrow;—vainly I had sought
  to borrow
From my books surcease of sorrow—sorrow for the
  lost Lenore—
For the rare and radiant maiden whom the angels
  name Lenore—
        Nameless *here* for evermore.

And the silken, sad, uncertain rustling of each purple curtain
Thrilled me—filled me with fantastic terrors never felt before;
So that now, to still the beating of my heart, I stood repeating
"'Tis some visiter entreating entrance at my chamber door—
Some late visiter entreating entrance at my chamber door;—
This it is and nothing more."

Presently my soul grew stronger; hesitating then no longer,
"Sir," said I, "or Madam, truly your forgiveness I implore;
But the fact is I was napping, and so gently you came rapping,
And so faintly you came tapping, tapping at my chamber door,
That I scarce was sure I heard you"—here I opened wide the door;—
Darkness there and nothing more.

Deep into that darkness peering, long I stood there wondering, fearing,

stanza continues

Doubting, dreaming dreams no mortal ever dared
  to dream before;
But the silence was unbroken, and the stillness gave
  no token,
And the only word there spoken was the whispered
  word, "Lenore?"
This I whispered, and an echo murmured back the
  word, "Lenore!"
                    Merely this and nothing more.

Back into the chamber turning, all my soul within
  me burning,
Soon again I heard a tapping somewhat louder than
  before.
"Surely," said I, "surely that is something at my
  window lattice;
Let me see, then, what thereat is, and this mystery
  explore—
Let my heart be still a moment and this mystery
  explore;—
                    'Tis the wind and nothing more!"

Open here I flung the shutter, when, with many a
  flirt and flutter,
In there stepped a stately Raven of the saintly days
  of yore;

stanza continues

Not the least obeisance made he; not a minute
stopped or stayed he;
But, with mien of lord or lady, perched above my
chamber door—
Perched upon a bust of Pallas just above my chamber
door—
Perched, and sat, and nothing more.

Then this ebony bird beguiling my sad fancy into
smiling,
By the grave and stern decorum of the countenance
it wore,
"Though thy crest be shorn and shaven, thou," I said,
"art sure no craven
Ghastly grim and ancient Raven wandering from
the Nightly shore—
Tell me what thy lordly name is on the Night's
Plutonian shore!"
Quoth the Raven "Nevermore."

Much I marvelled this ungainly fowl to hear discourse
so plainly,
Though its answer little meaning—little relevancy
bore;
For we cannot help agreeing that no living human
being

stanza continues

Ever yet was blessed with seeing bird above his
chamber door—
Bird or beast upon the sculptured bust above his
chamber door,
With such name as "Nevermore."

But the Raven, sitting lonely on the placid bust,
spoke only
That one word, as if his soul in that one word he
did outpour.
Nothing farther then he uttered—not a feather then
he fluttered—
Till I scarcely more than muttered "Other friends
have flown before—
On the morrow *he* will leave me, as my Hopes have
flown before."
Then the bird said "Nevermore."

Startled at the stillness broken by reply so aptly
spoken,
"Doubtless," said I, "what it utters is its only stock
and store
Caught from some unhappy master whom unmerciful
Disaster
Followed fast and followed faster till his songs one
burden bore—
Till the dirges of his Hope that melancholy burden
bore
Of 'Never—nevermore.'"

But the Raven still beguiling my sad fancy into
smiling,
Straight I wheeled a cushioned seat in front of bird,
and bust and door;
Then, upon the velvet sinking, I betook myself to
linking
Fancy unto fancy, thinking what this ominous bird
of yore—
What this grim, ungainly, ghastly, gaunt, and
ominous bird of yore
Meant in croaking "Nevermore."

This I sat engaged in guessing, but no syllable
expressing
To the fowl whose fiery eyes now burned into my
bosom's core;
This and more I sat divining, with my head at ease
reclining
On the cushion's velvet lining that the lamp-light
gloated o'er,
But whose velvet-violet lining with the lamp-light
gloating o'er,
She shall press, ah, nevermore!

Then, methought, the air grew denser, perfumed
from an unseen censer

stanza continues

Swung by seraphim whose foot-falls tinkled on the
tufted floor.
"Wretch," I cried, "thy God hath lent thee—by these
angels he hath sent thee
Respite—respite and nepenthe from thy memories
of Lenore;
Quaff, oh quaff this kind nepenthe and forget this
lost Lenore!"
Quoth the Raven "Nevermore."

"Prophet!" said I, "thing of evil!—prophet still, if
bird or devil!—
Whether Tempter sent, or whether tempest tossed
thee here ashore,
Desolate yet all undaunted, on this desert land
enchanted—
On this home by Horror haunted—tell me truly,
I implore—
Is there—*is* there balm in Gilead?—tell me—tell
me, I implore!"
Quoth the Raven "Nevermore."

"Prophet!" said I, "thing of evil!—prophet still, if
bird or devil!
By that Heaven that bends above us—by that God
we both adore—

stanza continues

Tell this soul with sorrow laden if, within the distant Aidenn,
It shall clasp a sainted maiden whom the angels name Lenore—
Clasp a rare and radiant maiden whom the angels name Lenore."
Quoth the Raven "Nevermore."

"Be that word our sign of parting, bird or fiend!" I shrieked, upstarting—
"Get thee back into the tempest and the Night's Plutonian shore!
Leave no black plume as a token of that lie thy soul hath spoken!
Leave my loneliness unbroken!—quit the bust above my door!
Take thy beak from out my heart, and take thy form from off my door!"
Quoth the Raven "Nevermore."

And the Raven, never flitting, still is sitting, *still* is sitting
On the pallid bust of Pallas just above my chamber door;
And his eyes have all the seeming of a demon's that is dreaming,

stanza continues

And the lamp-light o'er him streaming throws his shadow on the floor;
And my soul from out that shadow that lies floating on the floor
Shall be lifted—nevermore!

Ulalume—A Ballad

The skies they were ashen and sober;
    The leaves they were crispéd and sere—
    The leaves they were withering and sere:
It was night, in the lonesome October
    Of my most immemorial year:
It was hard by the dim lake of Auber,
    In the misty mid region of Weir—
It was down by the dank tarn of Auber,
    In the ghoul-haunted woodland of Weir.

Here once, through an alley Titanic,
    Of cypress, I roamed with my Soul—
    Of cypress, with Psyche, my Soul.
These were days when my heart was volcanic
    As the scoriac rivers that roll—
    As the lavas that restlessly roll—
Their sulphurous currents down Yaanek
    In the ultimate climes of the Pole—
That groan as they roll down Mount Yaanek
    In the realms of the Boreal Pole.

Our talk had been serious and sober,
    But our thoughts they were palsied and sere—
    Our memories were treacherous and sere;

stanza continues

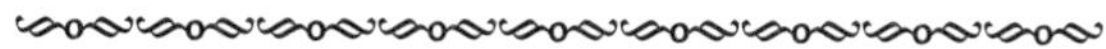

For we knew not the month was October,
    And we marked not the night of the year
    (Ah, night of all nights in the year!) —
We noted not the dim lake of Auber
    (Though once we had journeyed down here) —
We remembered not the dank tarn of Auber,
    Nor the ghoul-haunted woodland of Weir.

And now, as the night was senescent
    And star-dials pointed to morn —
    As the star-dials hinted of morn —
At the end of our path a liquescent
    And nebulous lustre was born,
Out of which a miraculous crescent
    Arose with a duplicate horn —
Astarte's bediamonded crescent
    Distinct with its duplicate horn.

And I said: "She is warmer than Dian;
    She rolls through an ether of sighs —
    She revels in a region of sighs.
She has seen that the tears are not dry on
    These cheeks, where the worm never dies,
And has come past the stars of the Lion,
    To point us the path to the skies —
    To the Lethean peace of the skies —

stanza continues

Come up, in despite of the Lion,
    To shine on us with her bright eyes—
Come up through the lair of the Lion,
    With love in her luminous eyes."

But Psyche, uplifting her finger,
    Said: "Sadly this star I mistrust—
    Her pallor I strangely mistrust:
Ah, hasten!—ah, let us not linger!
    Ah, fly!—let us fly!—for we must."
In terror she spoke, letting sink her
    Wings till they trailed in the dust—
In agony sobbed, letting sink her
    Plumes till they trailed in the dust—
    Till they sorrowfully trailed in the dust.

I replied: "This is nothing but dreaming:
    Let us on by this tremulous light!
    Let us bathe in this crystalline light!
Its Sibyllic splendor is beaming
    With Hope and in Beauty to-night:—
    See!—it flickers up the sky through the night!
Ah, we safely may trust to its gleaming,
    And be sure it will lead us aright—
We surely may trust to a gleaming,

stanza continues

That cannot but guide us aright,
Since it flickers up to Heaven through the night."

Thus I pacified Psyche and kissed her,
And tempted her out of her gloom—
And conquered her scruples and gloom;
And we passed to the end of the vista,
But were stopped by the door of a tomb—
By the door of a legended tomb;
And I said: "What is written, sweet sister,
On the door of this legended tomb?"
She replied: "Ulalume—Ulalume!—
'T is the vault of thy lost Ulalume!"

Then my heart it grew ashen and sober
As the leaves that were crispéd and sere—
As the leaves that were withering and sere;
And I cried: "It was surely October
On *this* very night of last year
That I journeyed—I journeyed down here!—
That I brought a dread burden down here—
On this night of all nights in the year,
Ah, what demon hath tempted me here?
Well I know, now, this dim lake of Auber—
This misty mid region of Weir—
Well I know, now, this dank tarn of Auber—
This ghoul-haunted woodland of Weir."

Said we, then—the two, then: "Ah, can it
    Have been that the woodlandish ghouls—
    The pitiful, the merciful ghouls—
To bar up our way and to ban it
    From the secret that lies in these wolds—
    From the thing that lies hidden in these wolds—
Have drawn up the spectre of a planet
    From the limbo of lunary souls—
This sinfully scintillant planet
    From the Hell of the planetary souls?"

The Kraken

Below the thunders of the upper deep;
Far, far beneath in the abysmal sea,
His ancient, dreamless, uninvaded sleep
The Kraken sleepeth: faintest sunlights flee
About his shadowy sides: above him swell
Huge sponges of millennial growth and height;
And far away into the sickly light,
From many a wondrous grot and secret cell
Unnumbered and enormous polypi
Winnow with giant fins the slumbering green.
There hath he lain for ages and will lie
Battening upon huge seaworms in his sleep,
Until the latter fire shall heat the deep;
Then once by men and angels to be seen,
In roaring he shall rise and on the surface die.

from The Lady of Shalott

Part I

On either side the river lie
Long fields of barley and of rye,
That clothe the wold and meet the sky;
And through the field the road runs by
        To many-towered Camelot;
And up and down the people go,
Gazing where the lilies blow
Round an island there below,
        The island of Shalott.

Willows whiten, aspens quiver,
Little breezes dusk and shiver
Through the wave that runs forever
By the island in the river
        Flowing down to Camelot.
Four grey walls, and four grey towers,
Overlook a space of flowers,
And the silent isle imbowers
        The Lady of Shalott.

By the margin, willow-veiled,
Slide the heavy barges trailed

stanza continues

By slow horses; and unhailed
The shallop flitteth silken-sailed
        Skimming down to Camelot:
But who hath seen her wave her hand?
Or at the casement seen her stand?
Or is she known in all the land,
        The Lady of Shalott?

Only reapers, reaping early
In among the bearded barley,
Hear a song that echoes cheerly
From the river winding clearly,
        Down to towered Camelot:
And by the moon the reaper weary,
Piling sheaves in uplands airy,
Listening, whispers "'Tis the fairy
        Lady of Shalott."

Part II

There she weaves by night and day
A magic web with colours gay.
She has heard a whisper say,
A curse is on her if she stay
        To look down to Camelot.
She knows not what the curse may be,
And so she weaveth steadily,
And little other care hath she,
        The Lady of Shalott.

And moving through a mirror clear
That hangs before her all the year,
Shadows of the world appear.
There she sees the highway near
        Winding down to Camelot:
There the river eddy whirls,
And there the surly village-churls,
And the red cloaks of market girls,
        Pass onward from Shalott.

Sometimes a troop of damsels glad,
An abbot on an ambling pad,
Sometimes a curly shepherd-lad,
Or long-haired page in crimson clad,
        Goes by to towered Camelot;
And sometimes through the mirror blue
The knights come riding two and two:
She hath no loyal knight and true,
        The Lady of Shalott.

But in her web she still delights
To weave the mirror's magic sights,
For often through the silent nights
A funeral, with plumes and lights
        And music, went to Camelot:
Or when the moon was overhead,
Came two young lovers lately wed;
"I am half sick of shadows," said
        The Lady of Shalott.

The Lotos-Eaters

"Courage!" he said, and pointed toward the land,
"This mounting wave will roll us shoreward soon."
In the afternoon they came unto a land
In which it seemèd always afternoon.
All round the coast the languid air did swoon,
Breathing like one that hath a weary dream.
Full-faced above the valley stood the moon;
And, like a downward smoke, the slender stream
Along the cliff to fall and pause and fall did seem.

A land of streams! some, like a downward smoke,
Slow-dropping veils of thinnest lawn, did go;
And some through wavering lights and shadows
  broke,
Rolling a slumbrous sheet of foam below.
They saw the gleaming river seaward flow
From the inner land: far off three mountain-tops,
Three silent pinnacles of agèd snow,
Stood sunset-flushed; and, dewed with showery
  drops,
Up-clomb the shadowy pine above the woven copse.

The charmèd sunset lingered low adown
In the red West; through mountain clefts the dale

stanza continues

Was seen far inland, and the yellow down
Bordered with palm, and many a winding vale
And meadow, set with slender galingale;
A land where all things always seemed the same!
And round about the keel with faces pale,
Dark faces pale against that rosy flame,
The mild-eyed melancholy Lotos-eaters came.

Branches they bore of that enchanted stem,
Laden with flower and fruit, whereof they gave
To each, but whoso did receive of them
And taste, to him the gushing of the wave
Far far away did seem to mourn and rave
On alien shores; and if his fellow spake,
His voice was thin, as voices from the grave;
And deep-asleep he seemed, yet all awake,
And music in his ears his beating heart did make.

They sat them down upon the yellow sand,
Between the sun and moon upon the shore;
And sweet it was to dream of Fatherland,
Of child, and wife, and slave; but evermore
Most weary seemed the sea, weary the oar,
Weary the wandering fields of barren foam.
Then some one said, "We will return no more;"
And all at once they sang, "Our island home
Is far beyond the wave; we will no longer roam."

continues

Choric Song

1

There is sweet music here that softer falls
Than petals from blown roses on the grass,
Or night-dews on still waters between walls
Of shadowy granite, in a gleaming pass;
Music that gentlier on the spirit lies,
Than tired eyelids upon tired eyes;
Music that brings sweet sleep down from the
  blissful skies.
Here are cool mosses deep,
And through the moss the ivies creep,
And in the stream the long-leaved flowers weep,
And from the craggy ledge the poppy hangs in sleep.

2

Why are we weighed upon with heaviness,
And utterly consumed with sharp distress,
While all things else have rest from weariness?
All things have rest: why should we toil alone,
We only toil, who are the first of things,
And make perpetual moan,
Still from one sorrow to another thrown;
Nor ever fold our wings,
And cease from wanderings,
Nor steep our brows in slumber's holy balm;

stanza continues

Nor harken what the inner spirit sings,
"There is no joy but calm!"
Why should we only toil, the roof and crown
  of things?

3

Lo! in the middle of the wood,
The folded leaf is wooed from out the bud
With winds upon the branch, and there
Grows green and broad, and takes no care,
Sun-steeped at noon, and in the moon
Nightly dew-fed; and turning yellow
Falls, and floats adown the air.
Lo! sweetened with the summer light,
The full-juiced apple, waxing over-mellow,
Drops in a silent autumn night.
All its allotted length of days,
The flower ripens in its place,
Ripens and fades, and falls, and hath no toil,
Fast-rooted in the fruitful soil.

4

Hateful is the dark-blue sky,
Vaulted o'er the dark-blue sea.
Death is the end of life; ah, why
Should life all labor be?
Let us alone. Time driveth onward fast

stanza continues

And in a little while our lips are dumb.
Let us alone. What is it that will last?
All things are taken from us, and become
Portions and parcels of the dreadful Past.
Let us alone. What pleasure can we have
To war with evil? Is there any peace
In ever climbing up the climbing wave?
All things have rest, and ripen toward the grave
In silence; ripen, fall, and cease:
Give us long rest or death, dark death, or
  dreamful ease.

5

How sweet it were, hearing the downward stream,
With half-shut eyes ever to seem
Falling asleep in a half-dream!
To dream and dream, like yonder amber light,
Which will not leave the myrrh-bush on the height;
To hear each other's whispered speech;
Eating the Lotos day by day,
To watch the crisping ripples on the beach,
And tender curving lines of creamy spray;
To lend our hearts and spirits wholly
To the influence of mild-minded melancholy;
To muse and brood and live again in memory,
With those old faces of our infancy
Heaped over with a mound of grass,
Two handfuls of white dust, shut in an urn of brass!

6

Dear is the memory of our wedded lives,
And dear the last embraces of our wives
And their warm tears: but all hath suffered change:
For surely now our household hearths are cold:
Our sons inherit us: our looks are strange:
And we should come like ghosts to trouble joy.
Or else the island princes over-bold
Have eat our substance, and the minstrel sings
Before them of the ten years' war in Troy,
And our great deeds, as half-forgotten things.
Is there confusion in the little isle?
Let what is broken so remain.
The Gods are hard to reconcile:
'Tis hard to settle order once again.
There *is* confusion worse than death,
Trouble on trouble, pain on pain,
Long labor unto agèd breath,
Sore tasks to hearts worn out by many wars
And eyes grown dim with gazing on the pilot-stars.

7

But, propt on beds of amaranth and moly,
How sweet (while warm airs lull us, blowing lowly)
With half-dropt eyelid still,
Beneath a heaven dark and holy,

stanza continues

To watch the long bright river drawing slowly
His waters from the purple hill—
To hear the dewy echoes calling
From cave to cave through the thick-twinèd vine—
To watch the emerald-colored water falling
Through many a woven acanthus-wreath divine!
Only to hear and see the far-off sparkling brine,
Only to hear were sweet, stretched out beneath
  the pine.

8

The Lotos blooms below the barren peak,
The Lotos blows by every winding creek;
All day the wind breathes low with mellower tone;
Through every hollow cave and alley lone
Round and round the spicy downs the yellow Lotos-
  dust is blown.
We have had enough of action, and of motion we,
Rolled to starboard, rolled to larboard, when the
  surge was seething free,
Where the wallowing monster spouted his foam-
  fountains in the sea.
Let us swear an oath, and keep it with an equal mind,
In the hollow Lotos-land to live and lie reclined
On the hills like Gods together, careless of mankind.
For they lie beside their nectar, and the bolts are
  hurled

stanza continues

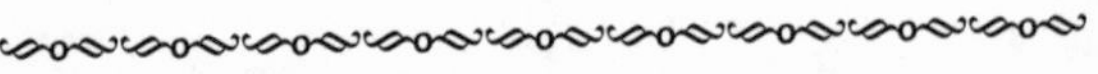

Far below them in the valleys, and the clouds are
lightly curled
Round their golden houses, girdled with the gleaming
world:
Where they smile in secret, looking over wasted
lands,
Blight and famine, plague and earthquake, roaring
deeps and fiery sands,
Clanging fights, and flaming towns, and sinking ships,
and praying hands.
But they smile, they find a music centered in a doleful
song
Steaming up, a lamentation and an ancient tale
of wrong,
Like a tale of little meaning though the words
are strong;
Chanted from an ill-used race of men that cleave
the soil,
Sow the seed, and reap the harvest with enduring
toil,
Storing yearly little dues of wheat, and wine and oil;
Till they perish and they suffer—some, 'tis
whispered—down in hell
Suffer endless anguish, others in Elysian valleys
dwell,
Resting weary limbs at last on beds of asphodel.

stanza continues

Surely, surely, slumber is more sweet than toil, the shore
Than labor in the deep mid-ocean, wind and wave and oar;
O, rest ye, brother mariners, we will not wander more.

Old Age in His Ailing

Old Age in his ailing
At youth will be railing
It scorns youth's regaling
Pooh-pooh it does, silly dream;
But me, the fool, save
From waxing so grave
As, reduced to skimmed milk, to slander the cream.

A Noiseless Patient Spider

A noiseless patient spider,
I mark'd where on a little promontory it stood
isolated,
Mark'd how to explore the vacant vast surrounding,
It launch'd forth filament, filament, filament, out
of itself,
Ever unreeling them, ever tirelessly speeding them.

And you O my soul where you stand,
Surrounded, detached, in measureless oceans of
space,
Ceaselessly musing, venturing, throwing, seeking
the spheres to connect them,
Till the bridge you will need be form'd, till the ductile
anchor hold,
Till the gossamer thread you fling catch
somewhere, O my soul.

WALT WHITMAN (1819–1892)

As I Ebb'd with the Ocean of Life

1

As I ebb'd with the ocean of life,
As I wended the shores I know,
As I walk'd where the ripples continually wash you
  Paumanok,
Where they rustle up hoarse and sibilant,
Where the fierce old mother endlessly cries for her
  castaways,
I musing late in the autumn day, gazing off
  southward,
Held by this electric self out of the pride of which I
  utter poems,
Was seiz'd by the spirit that trails in the lines
  underfoot,
The rim, the sediment that stands for all the water
  and all the land of the globe.

Fascinated, my eyes reverting from the south,
  dropt, to follow those slender windrows,
Chaff, straw, splinters of wood, weeds, and the
  sea-gluten,
Scum, scales from shining rocks, leaves of salt-
  lettuce, left by the tide,
Miles walking, the sound of breaking waves the
  other side of me,

stanza continues

Paumanok there and then as I thought the old
thought of likenesses,
These you presented to me you fish-shaped island,
As I wended the shores I know,
As I walk'd with that electric self seeking types.

2

As I wend to the shores I know not,
As I list to the dirge, the voices of men and women
wreck'd,
As I inhale the impalpable breezes that set in
upon me,
As the ocean so mysterious rolls toward me closer
and closer,
I too but signify at the utmost a little wash'd-up drift,
A few sands and dead leaves to gather,
Gather, and merge myself as part of the sands
and drift.

O baffled, balk'd, bent to the very earth,
Oppress'd with myself that I have dared to open
my mouth,
Aware now that amid all that blab whose echoes
recoil upon me I have not once had the least idea
who or what I am,

stanza continues

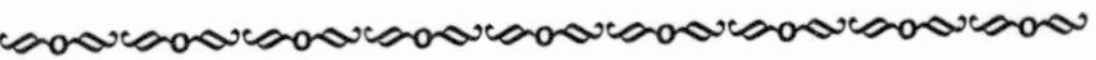

But that before all my arrogant poems the real Me
stands yet untouch'd, untold, altogether unreach'd,
Withdrawn far, mocking me with mock-
congratulatory signs and bows,
With peals of distant ironical laughter at every word
I have written,
Pointing in silence to these songs, and then to the
sand beneath.

I perceive I have not really understood any thing,
not a single object, and that no man ever can,
Nature here in sight of the sea taking advantage of
me to dart upon me and sting me,
Because I have dared to open my mouth to sing
at all.

3

You oceans both, I close with you,
We murmur alike reproachfully rolling sands and
drift, knowing not why,
These little shreds indeed standing for you and me
and all.

You friable shore with trails of debris,
You fish-shaped island, I take what is underfoot,
What is yours is mine my father.

stanza continues

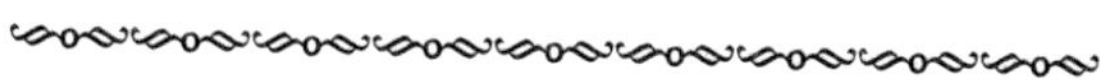

I too Paumanok,
I too have bubbled up, floated the measureless
float, and been wash'd on your shores,
I too am but a trail of drift and debris,
I too leave little wrecks upon you, you fish-
shaped island.

I throw myself upon your breast my father,
I cling to you so that you cannot unloose me,
I hold you so firm till you answer me something.

Kiss me my father,
Touch me with your lips as I touch those I love,
Breathe to me while I hold you close the secret of
the murmuring I envy.

4

Ebb, ocean of life, (the flow will return,)
Cease not your moaning you fierce old mother,
Endlessly cry for your castaways, but fear not,
deny not me,
Rustle not up so hoarse and angry against my feet
as I touch you or gather from you.
I mean tenderly by you and all,
I gather for myself and for this phantom looking
down where we lead, and following me and mine.

Me and mine, loose windrows, little corpses,
Froth, snowy white, and bubbles,
(See, from my dead lips the ooze excluding at last,
See, the prismatic colors glistening and rolling,)
Tufts or straw, sands, fragments,
Buoy'd hither from many moods, one contradicting another,
From the storm, the long calm, the darkness, the swell,
Musing, pondering, a breath, a briny tear, a dab of liquid or soil,
Up just as much out of fathomless workings fermented and thrown,
A limp blossom or two, torn, just as much over waves floating, drifted at random,
Just as much for us that sobbing dirge of Nature,
Just as much whence we come that blare of the cloud-trumpets,
We, capricious, brought hither we know not whence, spread out before you,
You up there walking or sitting,
Whoever you are, we too lie in drifts at your feet.

Unseen Buds

Unseen buds, infinite, hidden well,
Under the snow and ice, under the darkness, in
  every square or cubic inch,
Germinal, exquisite, in delicate lace, microscopic,
  unborn,
Like babes in wombs, latent, folded, compact,
  sleeping;
Billions of billions, and trillions of trillions of them
  waiting,
(On earth and in the sea—the universe—the stars
  there in the heavens,)
Urging slowly, surely forward, forming endless,
And waiting ever more, forever more behind.

When I Heard the Learn'd Astronomer

When I heard the learn'd astronomer,
When the proofs, the figures, were ranged in columns before me,
When I was shown the charts and diagrams, to add, divide, and measure them,
When I sitting heard the astronomer where he lectured with much applause in the lecture-room,
How soon unaccountable I became tired and sick,
Till rising and gliding out I wander'd off by myself,
In the mystical moist night-air, and from time to time,
Look'd up in perfect silence at the stars.

WALT WHITMAN (1819–1892)

The Sea-side Cave

At the dead of night by the side of the Sea
I met my gray-haired enemy, —
The glittering light of his serpent eye
Was all I had to see him by.

At the dead of night, and stormy weather
We went into a cave together, —
Into a cave by the side of the Sea,
And — he never came out with me!

The flower that up through the April mould
Comes like a miser dragging his gold,
Never made spot of earth so bright
As was the ground in the cave that night.

Dead of night, and stormy weather!
Who should see us going together
Under the black and dripping stone
Of the cave from whence I came alone!

Next day as my boy sat on my knee
He picked the gray hairs off from me,
And told with eyes brimful of fear
How a bird in the meadow near

Over her clay-built nest had spread
Sticks and leaves all bloody red,
Brought from a cave by the side of the Sea
Where some murdered man must be.

Dover Beach

The sea is calm tonight.
The tide is full, the moon lies fair
Upon the straits; on the French coast the light
Gleams and is gone; the cliffs of England stand,
Glimmering and vast, out in the tranquil bay.
Come to the window, sweet is the night-air!
Only, from the long line of spray
Where the sea meets the moon-blanched land,
Listen! you hear the grating roar
Of pebbles which the waves draw back, and fling,
At their return, up the high strand,
Begin, and cease, and then again begin,
With tremulous cadence slow, and bring
The eternal note of sadness in.

Sophocles long ago
Heard it on the Aegean, and it brought
Into his mind the turbid ebb and flow
Of human misery; we
Find also in the sound a thought,
Hearing it by this distant northern sea.

The Sea of Faith
Was once, too, at the full, and round earth's shore

stanza continues

Lay like the folds of a bright girdle furled.
But now I only hear
Its melancholy, long withdrawing roar,
Retreating, to the breath
Of the night-wind, down the vast edges drear
And naked shingles of the world.

Ah, love, let us be true
To one another! for the world, which seems
To lie before us like a land of dreams,
So various, so beautiful, so new,
Hath really neither joy, nor love, nor light,
Nor certitude, nor peace, nor help for pain;
And we are here as on a darkling plain
Swept with confused alarms of struggle and flight,
Where ignorant armies clash by night.

Lucifer in Starlight

On a starred night Prince Lucifer uprose.
Tired of his dark dominion, swung the fiend
Above the rolling ball, in cloud part screened,
Where sinners hugged their specter of repose.
Poor prey to his hot fit of pride were those.
And now upon his western wing he leaned,
Now his huge bulk o'er Afric's sands careened,
Now the black planet shadowed Arctic snows.
Soaring through wider zones that pricked his scars
With memory of the old revolt from Awe,
He reached a middle height, and at the stars,
Which are the brain of heaven, he looked, and sank.
Around the ancient track marched, rank on rank,
The army of unalterable law.

"Because I could not stop for Death,"

Because I could not stop for Death,
He kindly stopped for me;
The carriage held but just ourselves
And Immortality.

We slowly drove, he knew no haste,
And I had put away
My labor, and my leisure too,
For his civility.

We passed the school where children played
At wrestling in a ring;
We passed the fields of gazing grain,
We passed the setting sun.

We paused before a house that seemed
A swelling of the ground;
The roof was scarcely visible,
The cornice but a mound.

Since then 't is centuries; but each
Feels shorter than the day
I first surmised the horses' heads
Were toward eternity.

EMILY DICKINSON (1830–1886)

"Departed to the judgment,"

Departed to the judgment,
A mighty afternoon;
Great clouds like ushers leaning,
Creation looking on.

The flesh surrendered, cancelled,
The bodiless begun;
Two worlds, like audiences, disperse
And leave the soul alone.

"I dwell in Possibility—"

I dwell in Possibility—
A fairer House than Prose—
More numerous of Windows—
Superior—for Doors—

Of Chambers as the Cedars—
Impregnable of Eye—
And for an Everlasting Roof
The Gambrels of the Sky—

Of Visitors—the fairest—
For Occupation—This—
The spreading wide my narrow Hands
To gather Paradise—

"I felt a funeral in my brain,"

I felt a funeral in my brain,
  And mourners, to and fro,
Kept treading, treading, till it seemed
  That sense was breaking through.

And when they all were seated,
  A service like a drum
Kept beating, beating, till I thought
  My mind was going numb.

And then I heard them lift a box,
  And creak across my soul
With those same boots of lead, again.
  Then space began to toll

As all the heavens were a bell,
  And Being but an ear,
And I and silence some strange race,
  Wrecked, solitary, here.

"I never saw a moor,"

I never saw a moor,
I never saw the sea;
Yet know I how the heather looks,
And what a wave must be.

I never spoke with God,
Nor visited in heaven;
Yet certain am I of the spot
As if the chart were given.

EMILY DICKINSON (1830–1886)

"There's a certain slant of light,"

There's a certain slant of light,
On winter afternoons,
That oppresses, like the weight
Of cathedral tunes.

Heavenly hurt it gives us;
We can find no scar,
But internal difference
Where the meanings are.

None may teach it anything,
'T is the seal, despair,—
An imperial affliction
Sent us of the air.

When it comes, the landscape listens,
Shadows hold their breath;
When it goes, 't is like the distance
On the look of death.

"Passing away, saith the World, passing away:"

Passing away, saith the World, passing away:
Chances, beauty and youth sapped day by day:
Thy life never continueth in one stay.
Is the eye waxen dim, is the dark hair changing
to grey
That hath won neither laurel nor bay?
I shall clothe myself in Spring and bud in May:
Thou, root-stricken, shalt not rebuild thy decay
On my bosom for aye.
Then I answered: Yea.

Passing away, saith my Soul, passing away:
With its burden of fear and hope, of labour and play;
Hearken what the past doth witness and say:
Rust in thy gold, a moth is in thine array,
A canker is in thy bud, thy leaf must decay.
At midnight, at cockcrow, at morning, one certain
day
Lo the bridegroom shall come and shall not delay:
Watch thou and pray.
Then I answered: Yea.

continues

Passing away, saith my God, passing away:
Winter passeth after the long delay:
New grapes on the vine, new figs on the tender spray,
Turtle calleth turtle in Heaven's May.
Tho' I tarry, wait for Me, trust Me, watch and pray.
Arise, come away, night is past and lo it is day,
My love, My sister, My spouse, thou shalt hear
  Me say.
Then I answered: Yea.

from The City of Dreadful Night

He stood alone within the spacious square
  Declaiming from the central grassy mound,
With head uncovered and with streaming hair,
  As if large multitudes were gathered round:
A stalwart shape, the gestures full of might,
The glances burning with unnatural light:—

As I came through the desert thus it was,
As I came through the desert: All was black,
In heaven no single star, on earth no track;
A brooding hush without a stir or note,
The air so thick it clotted in my throat;
And thus for hours; then some enormous things
Swooped past with savage cries and clanking wings:
    But I strode on austere;
    No hope could have no fear.

As I came through the desert thus it was,
As I came through the desert: Eyes of fire
Glared at me throbbing with a starved desire;
The hoarse and heavy and carnivorous breath
Was hot upon me from deep jaws of death;
Sharp claws, swift talons, fleshless fingers cold
Plucked at me from the bushes, tried to hold:

stanza continues

But I strode on austere;
No hope could have no fear.

As I came through the desert thus it was,
As I came through the desert: Lo you, there,
That hillock burning with a brazen glare;
Those myriad dusky flames with points aglow
Which writhed and hissed and darted to and fro;
A Sabbath of the Serpents, heaped pell-mell
For Devil's roll-call and some *fête* of Hell:
Yet I strode on austere;
No hope could have no fear.

As I came through the desert thus it was,
As I came through the desert: Meteors ran
And crossed their javelins on the black sky-span;
The zenith opened to a gulf of flame,
The dreadful thunderbolts jarred earth's fixed frame:
The ground all heaved in waves of fire that surged
And weltered round me sole there unsubmerged:
Yet I strode on austere;
No hope could have no fear.

As I came through the desert thus it was,
As I came through the desert: Air once more,
And I was close upon a wild sea-shore;

stanza continues

Enormous cliffs arose on either hand,
The deep tide thundered up a league-broad strand;
White foambelts seethed there, wan spray swept
and flew;
The sky broke, moon and stars and clouds and blue:
And I strode on austere;
No hope could have no fear.

As I came through the desert thus it was,
As I came through the desert: On the left
The sun arose and crowned a broad crag-cleft;
There stopped and burned out black, except a rim,
A bleeding eyeless socket, red and dim;
Whereon the moon fell suddenly south-west,
And stood above the right-hand cliffs at rest:
Still I strode on austere;
No hope could have no fear.

As I came through the desert thus it was,
As I came through the desert: From the right
A shape came slowly with a ruddy light;
A woman with a red lamp in her hand,
Bareheaded and barefooted on that strand;
O desolation moving with such grace!
O anguish with such beauty in thy face!
I fell as on my bier,
Hope travailed with such fear.

continues

As I came through the desert thus it was,
As I came through the desert: I was twain,
Two selves distinct that cannot join again;
One stood apart and knew but could not stir,
And watched the other stark in swoon and her;
And she came on, and never turned aside,
Between such sun and moon and roaring tide:
        And as she came more near
        My soul grew mad with fear.

As I came through the desert thus it was,
As I came through the desert: Hell is mild
And piteous matched with that accursèd wild;
A large black sign was on her breast that bowed,
A broad black band ran down her snow-white
  shroud;
That lamp she held was her own burning heart,
Whose blood-drops trickled step by step apart;
        The mystery was clear;
        Mad rage had swallowed fear.

As I came through the desert thus it was,
As I came through the desert: By the sea
She knelt and bent above that senseless me;
Those lamp-drops fell upon my white brow there,
She tried to cleanse them with her tears and hair;

stanza continues

She murmured words of pity, love, and woe,
She heeded not the level rushing flow:
        And mad with rage and fear,
        I stood stonebound so near.

As I came through the desert thus it was,
As I came through the desert: When the tide
Swept up to her there kneeling by my side,
She clasped that corpse-like me, and they were borne
Away, and this vile me was left forlorn;
I know the whole sea cannot quench that heart,
Or cleanse that brow, or wash those two apart:
        They love; their doom is drear,
        Yet they nor hope nor fear;
        But I, what do I here?

God's Grandeur

The world is charged with the grandeur of God.
  It will flame out, like shining from shook foil;
  It gathers to a greatness, like the ooze of oil
Crushed. Why do men then now not reck his rod?
Generations have trod, have trod, have trod;
  And all is seared with trade; bleared, smeared
    with toil;
  And wears man's smudge and shares man's smell:
    the soil
Is bare now, nor can foot feel, being shod.

And for all this, nature is never spent;
  There lives the dearest freshness deep down
    things;
And though the last lights off the black West went
  Oh, morning, at the brown brink eastward,
    springs —
Because the Holy Ghost over the bent
  World broods with warm breast and with ah!
    bright wings.

Invictus

Out of the night that covers me,
  Black as the Pit from pole to pole,
I thank whatever gods may be
  For my unconquerable soul.

In the fell clutch of circumstance
  I have not winced nor cried aloud.
Under the bludgeonings of chance
  My head is bloody, but unbowed.

Beyond this place of wrath and tears
  Looms but the horror of the shade,
And yet the menace of the years
  Finds, and shall find me, unafraid.

It matters not how strait the gate,
  How charged with punishments the scroll,
I am the master of my fate;
  I am the captain of my soul.

I Shall Not Pass This Way Again

I shall not pass this way again—
  Although it bordered be with flowers,
  Although I rest in fragrant bowers,
    And hear the singing
    Of song-birds winging
To highest heaven their gladsome flight;
Though moons are full and stars are bright,
And winds and waves are softly sighing,
While leafy trees make low replying;
Though voices clear in joyous strain
Repeat a jubilant refrain;
Though rising suns their radiance throw
On summer's green and winter's snow,
In such rare splendor that my heart
Would ache from scenes like these to part;
    Though beauties heighten,
    And life-lights brighten,
And joys proceed from every pain,—
I shall not pass this way again.

Then let me pluck the flowers that blow,
And let me listen as I go
    To music rare
    That fills the air;

stanza continues

 EVA ROSE YORK (1858–?)

And let hereafter
Songs and laughter
Fill every pause along the way;
And to my spirit let me say:
"O soul, be happy; soon 'tis trod,
The path made thus for thee by God.
Be happy thou, and bless His name
By whom such marvellous beauty came."
And let no chance by me be lost
To kindness show at any cost.
I shall not pass this way again;
Then let me now relieve some pain,
Remove some barrier from the road,
Or brighten some one's heavy load;
A helping hand to this one lend,
Then turn some other to befriend.

O God, forgive
That now I live
As if I might, sometime, return
To bless the weary ones that yearn
For help and comfort every day,—
For there be such along the way.
O God, forgive that I have seen
The beauty only, have not been
Awake to sorrow such as this;
That I have drunk the cup of bliss

stanza continues

Remembering not that those there be
Who drink the dregs of misery.

I love the beauty of the scene,
Would roam again o'er fields so green;
But since I may not, let me spend
My strength for others to the end,—
For those who tread on rock and stone,
And bear their burdens all alone,
Who loiter not in leafy bowers,
Nor hear the birds nor pluck the flowers.
A larger kindness give to me,
A deeper love and sympathy;
    Then, O, one day
    May someone say—
Remembering a lessened pain—
"Would she could pass this way again."

The Wild Ride

I hear in my heart, I hear in its ominous pulses
All day, on the road, the hoofs of invisible horses,
All night, from their stalls, the importunate pawing and neighing.

Let cowards and laggards fall back! but alert to the saddle
Weather-worn and abreast, go men of our galloping legion,
With a stirrup-cup each to the lily of women that loves him.

The trail is through dolour and dread, over crags and morasses;
There are shapes by the way, there are things that appal or entice us:
What odds? We are Knights of the Grail, we are vowed to the riding.

Thought's self is a vanishing wing, and joy is a cobweb,
And friendship a flower in the dust, and glory a sunbeam:
Not here is our prize, nor, alas! after these our pursuing.

continues

A dipping of plumes, a tear, a shake of the bridle,
A passing salute to this world and her pitiful beauty:
We hurry with never a word in the track of our
  fathers.

(I hear in my heart, I hear in its ominous pulses
All day, on the road, the hoofs of invisible horses,
All night, from their stalls, the importunate pawing
  and neighing.)

We spur to a land of no name, out-racing the storm-
  wind;
We leap to the infinite dark like sparks from the anvil.
Thou leadest, O God! All's well with Thy troopers
  that follow.

The Second Coming

Turning and turning in the widening gyre
The falcon cannot hear the falconer;
Things fall apart; the centre cannot hold;
Mere anarchy is loosed upon the world,
The blood-dimmed tide is loosed, and everywhere
The ceremony of innocence is drowned;
The best lack all conviction, while the worst
Are full of passionate intensity.

Surely some revelation is at hand;
Surely the Second Coming is at hand:
The Second Coming! Hardly are those words out
When a vast image out of *Spiritus Mundi*
Troubles my sight: somewhere in sands of the
desert
A shape with lion body and the head of a man,
A gaze blank and pitiless as the sun,
Is moving its slow thighs, while all about it
Reel shadows of the indignant desert birds.
The darkness drops again; but now I know
That twenty centuries of stony sleep
Were vexed to nightmare by a rocking cradle,
And what rough beast, its hour come round at last,
Slouches towards Bethlehem to be born?

A Man Said to the Universe

A man said to the universe:
"Sir, I exist!"
"However," replied the universe,
"The fact has not created in me
A sense of obligation."

Black Riders Came from the Sea

Black riders came from the sea.
There was clang and clang of spear and shield,
And clash and clash of hoof and heel,
Wild shouts and the wave of hair
In the rush upon the wind:
Thus the ride of Sin.

In the Desert

In the desert
I saw a creature, naked, bestial,
Who, squatting upon the ground,
Held his heart in his hands,
And ate of it.
I said, "Is it good, friend?"
"It is bitter—bitter," he answered,
"But I like it
Because it is bitter,
And because it is my heart."

from The Waste Land

I. The Burial of the Dead

April is the cruellest month, breeding
Lilacs out of the dead land, mixing
Memory and desire, stirring
Dull roots with spring rain.
Winter kept us warm, covering
Earth in forgetful snow, feeding
A little life with dried tubers.
Summer surprised us, coming over the
  Starnbergersee
With a shower of rain; we stopped in the colonnade,
And went on in sunlight, into the Hofgarten,
And drank coffee, and talked for an hour.
Bin gar keine Russin, stamm' aus Litauen,
  echt deutsch.
And when we were children, staying at the
  arch-duke's,
My cousin's, he took me out on a sled,
And I was frightened. He said, Marie,
Marie, hold on tight. And down we went.
In the mountains, there you feel free.
I read, much of the night, and go south in the winter.

continues

What are the roots that clutch, what branches grow
Out of this stony rubbish? Son of man,
You cannot say, or guess, for you know only
A heap of broken images, where the sun beats,
And the dead tree gives no shelter, the cricket
no relief,
And the dry stone no sound of water. Only
There is shadow under this red rock,
(Come in under the shadow of this red rock),
And I will show you something different from either
Your shadow at morning striding behind you
Or your shadow at evening rising to meet you;
I will show you fear in a handful of dust.
Frisch weht der Wind
Der Heimat zu
Mein Irisch Kind,
Wo weilest du?
"You gave me hyacinths first a year ago;
"They called me the hyacinth girl."
—Yet when we came back, late, from the hyacinth
garden,
Your arms full, and your hair wet, I could not
Speak, and my eyes failed, I was neither
Living nor dead, and I knew nothing,
Looking into the heart of light, the silence.
Oed' und leer das Meer.

Madame Sosostris, famous clairvoyante,
Had a bad cold, nevertheless
Is known to be the wisest woman in Europe,
With a wicked pack of cards. Here, said she,
Is your card, the drowned Phoenician Sailor,
(Those are pearls that were his eyes. Look!)
Here is Belladonna, the Lady of the Rocks,
The lady of situations.
Here is the man with three staves, and here the
Wheel,
And here is the one-eyed merchant, and this card,
Which is blank, is something he carries on his back,
Which I am forbidden to see. I do not find
The Hanged Man. Fear death by water.
I see crowds of people, walking round in a ring.
Thank you. If you see dear Mrs. Equitone,
Tell her I bring the horoscope myself:
One must be so careful these days.

Unreal city,
Under the brown fog of a winter dawn,
A crowd flowed over London Bridge, so many,
I had not thought death had undone so many.
Sighs, short and infrequent, were exhaled,
And each man fixed his eyes before his feet.
Flowed up the hill and down King William Street,
To where Saint Mary Woolnoth kept the hours

stanza continues

With a dead sound on the final stroke of nine.
There I saw one I knew, and stopped him, crying:
"Stetson!
"You who were with me in the ships at Mylae!
"That corpse you planted last year in your garden,
"Has it begun to sprout? Will it bloom this year?
"Or has the sudden frost disturbed its bed?
"O keep the Dog far hence, that's friend to men,
"Or with his nails he'll dig it up again!
"You! hypocrite lecteur!—mon semblable,—
mon frère!"

I Have a Rendezvous with Death

I have a rendezvous with Death
At some disputed barricade
When Spring comes round with rustling shade
And apple blossoms fill the air.
I have a rendezvous with Death
When Spring brings back blue days and fair.

It may be he shall take my hand
And lead me into his dark land
And close my eyes and quench my breath;
It may be I shall pass him still.
I have a rendezvous with Death
On some scarred slope of battered hill,
When Spring comes round again this year
And the first meadow flowers appear.

God knows 'twere better to be deep
Pillowed in silk and scented down,
Where love throbs out in blissful sleep,
Pulse nigh to pulse, and breath to breath,
Where hushed awakenings are dear . . .
But I've a rendezvous with Death
At midnight in some flaming town,
When Spring trips north again this year,
And I to my pledged word am true,
I shall not fail that rendezvous.

Renascence

All I could see from where I stood
Was three long mountains and a wood;
I turned and looked the other way,
And saw three islands in a bay.
So with my eyes I traced the line
Of the horizon, thin and fine,
Straight around till I was come
Back to where I'd started from;
And all I saw from where I stood
Was three long mountains and a wood.
Over these things I could not see:
These were the things that bounded me;
And I could touch them with my hand,
Almost, I thought, from where I stand.
And all at once things seemed so small
My breath came short, and scarce at all.
But, sure, the sky is big, I said;
Miles and miles above my head;
So here upon my back I'll lie
And look my fill into the sky.
And so I looked, and, after all,
The sky was not so very tall.
The sky, I said, must somewhere stop,
And—sure enough!—I see the top!

stanza continues

The sky, I thought, is not so grand;
I 'most could touch it with my hand!
And reaching up my hand to try,
I screamed to feel it touch the sky.
I screamed, and—lo!—Infinity
Came down and settled over me;
Forced back my scream into my chest,
Bent back my arm upon my breast,
And, pressing of the Undefined
The definition on my mind,
Held up before my eyes a glass
Through which my shrinking sight did pass
Until it seemed I must behold
Immensity made manifold;
Whispered to me a word whose sound
Deafened the air for worlds around,
And brought unmuffled to my ears
The gossiping of friendly spheres,
The creaking of the tented sky,
The ticking of Eternity.
I saw and heard and knew at last
The How and Why of all things, past,
And present, and forevermore.
The Universe, cleft to the core,
Lay open to my probing sense
That, sick'ning, I would fain pluck thence

stanza continues

But could not,—nay! But needs must suck
At the great wound, and could not pluck
My lips away till I had drawn
All venom out.—Ah, fearful pawn!
For my omniscience paid I toll
In infinite remorse of soul.
All sin was of my sinning, all
Atoning mine, and mine the gall
Of all regret. Mine was the weight
Of every brooded wrong, the hate
That stood behind each envious thrust,
Mine every greed, mine every lust.
And all the while for every grief,
Each suffering, I craved relief
With individual desire,—
Craved all in vain! And felt fierce fire
About a thousand people crawl;
Perished with each,—then mourned for all!
A man was starving in Capri;
He moved his eyes and looked at me;
I felt his gaze, I heard his moan,
And knew his hunger as my own.
I saw at sea a great fog bank
Between two ships that struck and sank;
A thousand screams the heavens smote;
And every scream tore through my throat.

stanza continues

No hurt I did not feel, no death
That was not mine; mine each last breath
That, crying, met an answering cry
From the compassion that was I.
All suffering mine, and mine its rod;
Mine, pity like the pity of God.
Ah, awful weight! Infinity
Pressed down upon the finite Me!
My anguished spirit, like a bird,
Beating against my lips I heard;
Yet lay the weight so close about
There was no room for it without.
And so beneath the weight lay I
And suffered death, but could not die.

Long had I lain thus, craving death,
When quietly the earth beneath
Gave way, and inch by inch, so great
At last had grown the crushing weight,
Into the earth I sank till I
Full six feet under ground did lie,
And sank no more,—there is no weight
Can follow here, however great.
From off my breast I felt it roll,
And as it went my tortured soul
Burst forth and fled in such a gust
That all about me swirled the dust.

continues

Deep in the earth I rested now;
Cool is its hand upon the brow
And soft its breast beneath the head
Of one who is so gladly dead.
And all at once, and over all
The pitying rain began to fall;
I lay and heard each pattering hoof
Upon my lowly, thatchèd roof,
And seemed to love the sound far more
Than ever I had done before.
For rain it hath a friendly sound
To one who's six feet under ground;
And scarce the friendly voice or face:
A grave is such a quiet place.

The rain, I said, is kind to come
And speak to me in my new home.
I would I were alive again
To kiss the fingers of the rain,
To drink into my eyes the shine
Of every slanting silver line,
To catch the freshened, fragrant breeze
From drenched and dripping apple-trees.
For soon the shower will be done,
And then the broad face of the sun
Will laugh above the rain-soaked earth
Until the world with answering mirth

stanza continues

Shakes joyously, and each round drop
Rolls, twinkling, from its grass-blade top.
How can I bear it; buried here,
While overhead the sky grows clear
And blue again after the storm?
O, multi-colored, multiform,
Beloved beauty over me,
That I shall never, never see
Again! Spring-silver, autumn-gold,
That I shall never more behold!
Sleeping your myriad magics through,
Close-sepulchred away from you!
O God, I cried, give me new birth,
And put me back upon the earth!
Upset each cloud's gigantic gourd
And let the heavy rain, down-poured
In one big torrent, set me free,
Washing my grave away from me!

I ceased; and through the breathless hush
That answered me, the far-off rush
Of herald wings came whispering
Like music down the vibrant string
Of my ascending prayer, and—crash!
Before the wild wind's whistling lash
The startled storm-clouds reared on high
And plunged in terror down the sky,

stanza continues

And the big rain in one black wave
Fell from the sky and struck my grave.
I know not how such things can be;
I only know there came to me
A fragrance such as never clings
To aught save happy living things;
A sound as of some joyous elf
Singing sweet songs to please himself,
And, through and over everything,
A sense of glad awakening.
The grass, a-tiptoe at my ear,
Whispering to me I could hear;
I felt the rain's cool finger-tips
Brushed tenderly across my lips,
Laid gently on my sealed sight,
And all at once the heavy night
Fell from my eyes and I could see,—
A drenched and dripping apple-tree,
A last long line of silver rain,
A sky grown clear and blue again.
And as I looked a quickening gust
Of wind blew up to me and thrust
Into my face a miracle
Of orchard-breath, and with the smell,—
I know not how such things can be!—
I breathed my soul back into me.

stanza continues

Ah! Up then from the ground sprang I
And hailed the earth with such a cry
As is not heard save from a man
Who has been dead, and lives again.
About the trees my arms I wound;
Like one gone mad I hugged the ground;
I raised my quivering arms on high;
I laughed and laughed into the sky,
Till at my throat a strangling sob
Caught fiercely, and a great heart-throb
Sent instant tears into my eyes;
O God, I cried, no dark disguise
Can e'er hereafter hide from me
Thy radiant identity!
Thou canst not move across the grass
But my quick eyes will see Thee pass,
Nor speak, however silently,
But my hushed voice will answer Thee.
I know the path that tells Thy way
Through the cool eve of every day;
God, I can push the grass apart
And lay my finger on Thy heart!

The world stands out on either side
No wider than the heart is wide;
Above the world is stretched the sky, —
No higher than the soul is high.

stanza continues

The heart can push the sea and land
Farther away on either hand;
The soul can split the sky in two,
And let the face of God shine through.
But East and West will pinch the heart
That can not keep them pushed apart;
And he whose soul is flat—the sky
Will cave in on him by and by.

Proem: To Brooklyn Bridge

from *THE BRIDGE*

How many dawns, chill from his rippling rest
The seagull's wings shall dip and pivot him,
Shedding white rings of tumult, building high
Over the chained bay waters Liberty—

Then, with inviolate curve, forsake our eyes
As apparitional as sails that cross
Some page of figures to be filed away;
—Till elevators drop us from our day . . .

I think of cinemas, panoramic sleights
With multitudes bent toward some flashing scene
Never disclosed, but hastened to again,
Foretold to other eyes on the same screen;

And Thee, across the harbor, silver-paced
As though the sun took step of thee, yet left
Some motion ever unspent in thy stride—
Implicitly thy freedom staying thee!

Out of some subway scuttle, cell or loft
A bedlamite speeds to thy parapets,

stanza continues

Tilting there momently, shrill shirt ballooning,
A jest falls from the speechless caravan.

Down Wall, from girder into street noon leaks,
A rip-tooth of the sky's acetylene;
All afternoon the cloud-flown derricks turn . . .
Thy cables breathe the North Atlantic still.

And obscure as that heaven of the Jews,
Thy guerdon . . . Accolade thou dost bestow
Of anonymity time cannot raise:
Vibrant reprieve and pardon thou dost show.

O harp and altar, of the fury fused,
(How could mere toil align thy choiring strings!)
Terrific threshold of the prophet's pledge,
Prayer of pariah, and the lover's cry—

Again the traffic lights that skim thy swift
Unfractioned idiom, immaculate sigh of stars,
Beading thy path—condense eternity:
And we have seen night lifted in thine arms.

Under thy shadow by the piers I waited;
Only in darkness is thy shadow clear.
The City's fiery parcels all undone,
Already snow submerges an iron year . . .

O Sleepless as the river under thee,
Vaulting the sea, the prairies' dreaming sod,
Unto us lowliest sometime sweep, descend
And of the curveship lend a myth to God.

from Howl

II

What sphinx of cement and aluminum bashed open
their skulls and ate up their brains and
imagination?
Moloch! Solitude! Filth! Ugliness! Ashcans and
unobtainable dollars! Children screaming under
the stairways! Boys sobbing in armies! Old men
weeping in the parks!
Moloch! Moloch! Nightmare of Moloch! Moloch
the loveless! Mental Moloch! Moloch the heavy
judger of men!
Moloch the incomprehensible prison! Moloch the
crossbone soulless jailhouse and Congress of
sorrows! Moloch whose buildings are judgment!
Moloch the vast stone of war! Moloch the
stunned governments!
Moloch whose mind is pure machinery! Moloch
whose blood is running money! Moloch whose
fingers are ten armies! Moloch whose breast is a
cannibal dynamo! Moloch whose ear is a
smoking tomb!
Moloch whose eyes are a thousand blind windows!
Moloch whose skyscrapers stand in the long
streets like endless Jehovahs! Moloch whose

factories dream and croak in the fog! Moloch
whose smokestacks and antennae crown the cities!
Moloch whose love is endless oil and stone!
Moloch whose soul is electricity and banks!
Moloch whose poverty is the specter of genius!
Moloch whose fate is a cloud of sexless hydrogen!
Moloch whose name is the Mind!
Moloch in whom I sit lonely! Moloch in whom I
dream Angels! Crazy in Moloch! Cocksucker in
Moloch! Lacklove and manless in Moloch!
Moloch who entered my soul early! Moloch in
whom I am a consciousness without a body!
Moloch who frightened me out of my natural
ecstasy! Moloch whom I abandon! Wake up in
Moloch! Light streaming out of the sky!
Moloch! Moloch! Robot apartments! invisible
suburbs! skeleton treasuries! blind capitals!
demonic industries! spectral nations! invincible
madhouses! granite cocks! monstrous bombs!
They broke their backs lifting Moloch to Heaven!
Pavements, trees, radios, tons! lifting the city to
Heaven which exists and is everywhere about us!
Visions! omens! hallucinations! miracles! ecstasies!
gone down the American river!
Dreams! adorations! illuminations! religions! the
whole boatload of sensitive bullshit!

continues

Breakthroughs! over the river! flips and crucifixions!
  gone down the flood! Highs! Epiphanies!
  Despairs! Ten years' animal screams and suicides!
  Minds! New loves! Mad generation! down on the
  rocks of Time!
Real holy laughter in the river! They saw it all!
  the wild eyes! the holy yells! They bade farewell!
  They jumped off the roof! to solitude! waving!
  carrying flowers! Down to the river! into
  the street!

Index of Authors

Dante Alighieri, 5
Matthew Arnold, 202
The Bible, 1
William Blake, 84, 85, 87, 88, 89, 94, 95
Robert Burns, 97
Lord Byron, 125
Alice Cary, 200
Samuel Taylor Coleridge, 109, 112
William Collins, 74
William Cowper, 78
Hart Crane, 243
Stephen Crane, 226, 227, 228
Richard Crashaw, 56
Emily Dickinson, 205, 206, 207, 208, 209, 210
John Donne, 24, 25, 27, 29, 31
T. S. Eliot, 229
Ralph Waldo Emerson, 146, 147, 149
Allen Ginsberg, 246
Thomas Gray, 68
Louise Imogen Guiney, 223
William Ernest Henley, 219
George Herbert, 42, 45, 46
Homer, 2
Gerard Manley Hopkins, 218
John Keats, 138, 139, 142
Henry King, 34
Henry Wadsworth Longfellow, 151, 154
Herman Melville, 191
George Meredith, 204
Edna St. Vincent Millay, 234
John Milton, 47, 54
Edgar Allan Poe, 157, 159, 164, 173
Francis Quarles, 39
Sir Walter Ralegh, 11
Christina Rossetti, 211
Rumi, 4
Alan Seeger, 233
William Shakespeare, 20, 21, 23
Percy Bysshe Shelley, 128, 132
Robert Southwell, 18
Edmund Spenser, 14
Alfred, Lord Tennyson, 178, 179, 182
James Thomson, 213

Thomas Traherne, 64
Henry Vaughan, 57, 59, 62
Phillis Wheatley, 81, 82
Walt Whitman, 192, 193, 198, 199
William Wordsworth, 99, 108
William Butler Yeats, 225
Eva Rose York, 220

Index of First Lines

A man said to the universe: 226
A noiseless patient spider, 192
Accept, thou shrine of my dead saint, 34
Ah! sunflower, weary of time, 88
All I could see from where I stood 234
All kings, and all their favorites, 27
April is the cruellest month, breeding 229
As I ebb'd with the ocean of life, 193
As I in hoary winter's night stood shivering in the snow, 18
As once, if not with light regard, 74
At the dead of night by the side of the Sea 200
Attend my lays, ye ever honour'd nine, 81
Because I could not stop for Death, 205
Below the thunders of the upper deep; 178
Black riders came from the sea. 227
"Courage!" he said, and pointed toward the land, 182
Daughters of Time, the hypocritic Days, 146
Deare love, for nothing lesse then thee 29
Death, be not proud, though some have called thee 24

Departed to the judgment, 206
Eternity appear'd above them as One Man, enfolded 87
Gaily bedight, 157
Give me my scallop-shell of quiet, 11
Go and catch a falling star, 25
Good-bye, proud world! I'm going home: 149
Grim monarch! see, deprived of vital breath 82
Hail to thee, blithe Spirit! 132
Happy those early days! when I 57
He stood alone within the spacious square 213
Hear the sledges with the bells— 159
Hence vain deluding Joys, 47
How like an Angel came I down! 64
How many dawns, chill from his rippling rest 243
I dwell in Possibility— 207
I felt a funeral in my brain, 208
I have a rendezvous with Death 233
I hear in my heart, I hear in its ominous pulses 223
I never saw a moor, 209
I saw Eternity the other night 59
I see the Fourfold Man; the Humanity in deadly sleep, 85

I shall not pass this way again— 220
I wander thro' each charter'd street, 94
I was angry with my friend; 84
In Mather's Magnalia Christi, 154
In the desert 228
In Xanadu did Kubla Khan 109
Is there, for honest poverty, 97
"Is this the Region, this the Soil, the Clime," 54
It is an ancient Mariner 112
Lord, who createdst man in wealth and store, 45
"Mine and yours; 147
My heart aches, and a drowsy numbness pains 142
Not marble, nor the gilded monuments 20
Obscurest night involved the sky, 78
Old Age in his ailing 191
On a starred night Prince Lucifer uprose. 204
On either side the river lie 179
Once upon a midnight dreary, while I pondered, weak and weary, 164
Out of the night that covers me, 219
Passing away, saith the World, passing away: 211
Pour, cupbearer, the wine of the invisible, 4
The awful shadow of some unseen Power 128

The curfew tolls the knell of parting day, 68
The day is done, and the darkness 151
The sea is calm tonight. 202
The skies they were ashen and sober; 173
The world is charged with the grandeur of God. 218
The world is too much with us; late and soon, 108
There was a time when meadow, grove, and stream, 99
There's a certain slant of light, 210
They are all gone into the world of light! 62
Thou still unravished bride of quietness, 139
"Through me the way is to the city dolent; 5
"Thus in a tide of tears our sorrows flow, 2
Titan! to whose immortal eyes 125
To be, or not to be, that is the question: 21
To every thing there is a season, and a time to every purpose under the heaven: 1
To see a World in a grain of sand, 89
To these, whom Death again did wed, 56
To-morrow, and to-morrow, and to-morrow, 23
Turning and turning in the widening gyre 225
Tyger, Tyger, burning bright, 95
Unseen buds, infinite, hidden well, 198

Vnto this place when as the Elfin Knight 14
What sphinx of cement and aluminum bashed open their skulls and ate up their brains and imagination? 246
When first thou didst entice to thee my heart, 42
When God at first made man, 46
When I have fears that I may cease to be 138
When I heard the learn'd astronomer, 199
Where, like a pillow on a bed, 31
Why dost thou shade thy lovely face? O why 39

Acknowledgments

"Proem: To Brooklyn Bridge," by Hart Crane. From COMPLETE POEMS OF HART CRANE by Hart Crane, edited by Marc Simon. Copyright 1933, 1958, 1966 by Liveright Publishing Corporation. Copyright © 1986 by Marc Simon. Used by permission of Liveright Publishing Corporation.

"I dwell in possibility," by Emily Dickinson. Reprinted by permission of the publishers and the Trustees of Amherst College from THE POEMS OF EMILY DICKINSON, Thomas H. Johnson, ed., Cambridge, Mass.: The Belknap Press of Harvard University Press, Copyright © 1951, 1955, 1979 by the President and Fellows of Harvard College.

"Howl: Part II," by Allen Ginsberg. Copyright © 1955 by Allen Ginsberg. Reprinted by permission of HarperCollins Publishers Inc.

"Lift Now the Lid of the Jar of Heaven," by Rumi. From TEACHINGS OF RUMI, edited by Andrew Harvey. Copyright © 1999 by Andrew Harvey. Reprinted by arrangement with Shambhala Publications, Inc., Boston, www.shambhala.com.